Canadian Living
Pasta & Noodles

BY THE CANADIAN LIVING TEST KITCHEN

JUNIPER
PUBLISHING
A Quebecor Media Corporation

From Our Test Kitchen

I can't think of a single person who doesn't include a pasta or noodle dish in their list of top five comfort foods. Growing up, my favourite dinner was spaghetti with meat sauce. And—surprise, surprise—this dish still makes frequent appearances on my dinner table today. I'm not the only one who thinks this, either. In households across Canada, noodles hold an important place on our tables, whether they're tucked under saucy meatballs or stir-fried with crisp vegetables and tofu.

It's easy to see why pasta is such a winning dinner option. A simple mix of flour and water creates an ingredient that's pantry-friendly, affordable, nutritious, filling and versatile. Better yet, pasta cooks in a flash (often 10 minutes or less), making it an excellent ingredient for nights when you're strapped for time. Plus, noodles come in such a variety of shapes and sizes that you're bound to find something to please even the pickiest eater.

My mother's meat sauce recipe was a little simpler than mine, both because my cooking repertoire is a bit more varied and because my mum didn't have access to the array of ingredients available in modern supermarkets. Today, pasta can be the base for any number of flavourful dishes, rather than just a starch to toss with tomato sauce (though I still love a good tomato sauce). That's the beauty of pasta: It can be as simple or as fancy as you like, depending on what you add and how much time you have to cook.

In these pages, you'll find 101 Tested-Till-Perfect pasta, noodle and sauce recipes. Some are cozy and familiar, such as Creamy Chicken and Mushroom Pasta (page 16) or The Ultimate Macaroni and Cheese (page 90). Some are adventurous, such as Ricotta Gnocchi With Sautéed Beets (page 84) or Braised Chinese Beef and Daikon With Noodles (page 142). Plenty of other recipes are somewhere in between, providing you with lots of dinner options. I'm positive one of these inspired dishes will end up on your top-five list, too.

Eat well and enjoy!

ANNABELLE WAUGH
FOOD DIRECTOR

Thai Chicken Noodle Bowl
page 126

"Noodles come in such a variety of shapes and sizes that you're bound to find something to please even the pickiest eater."

The Ultimate Lasagna
page 99

Contents

PERFECT PASTA & NOODLES

FOLLOW THE INSTRUCTIONS

Recipes from the Canadian Living Test Kitchen usually say to cook pasta according to the package instructions because no two noodles are exactly alike. For example, even though two brands may both be labelled "spaghetti" or "rotini," they may be very slightly different in size or contain different types of wheat or other grains. Either of those factors will change the cooking time.

TASTE & TASTE AGAIN

While the package instructions will give you an estimated cooking time, your best tool for judging doneness is your teeth. Once the pasta has cooked for five minutes, try a noodle roughly every minute thereafter until the pasta reaches your desired texture. To us, al dente is perfect: a noodle should yield easily to the bite but still be firm in the centre (never mushy).

HOW TO SWAP FRESH PASTA FOR DRIED

To substitute fresh pasta for dried, use about one-and-a-half times the quantity called for, and cook it according to the package instructions. Fresh pasta cooks in a fraction of the time it takes to cook dried pasta.

THE Ready-for-Pasta GROCERY LIST

- ○ Olive oil
- ○ Canned tomatoes, tomato sauce and tomato paste
- ○ Bottled strained tomatoes, also called passata
- ○ Onions and garlic
- ○ Fresh herbs, such as parsley, basil, oregano and more
- ○ Broth, such as chicken and vegetable
- ○ Olives and marinated artichokes
- ○ Dried and fresh mushrooms
- ○ Jarred roasted red peppers
- ○ Sun-dried tomatoes, dry-packed and/or oil-packed
- ○ Milk or evaporated milk
- ○ Cheese, such as Parmesan, Romano, fresh mozzarella, feta and more
- ○ Canned clams, tuna, salmon and anchovies
- ○ Bacon, pancetta or prosciutto
- ○ Frozen scallops or shrimp

PASTA & SAUCE PAIRINGS

You can toss your favourite pasta shape with whatever sauce you like—there are no hard-and-fast rules—but certain pasta shapes and sauces work particularly well together.

CHUNKY VEGETABLE SAUCES	CHEESE SAUCES	CREAM & BUTTER SAUCES	PESTOS & OIL-BASED SAUCES	MEAT SAUCES	SOUPS
Use pasta shapes that have crannies and crevices to catch and hold the vegetables.	Use small pasta shapes with lots of surface area.	You need only a small amount of these rich sauces to cover long noodles evenly.	These sauces are excellent for keeping long thin pastas from clumping together.	In Northern Italy, wide fresh egg noodles are used; in Southern Italy, it's small dried pasta shapes.	Choose small pasta according to the amount you want in each spoonful. The smaller the pieces, the more in each bite.
Try: FUSILLI ORECCHIETTE CONCHIGLIE	FUSILLI FARFALLE MACARONI PENNE SHELLS	LINGUINE FETTUCCINE	BUCATINI LINGUINE SPAGHETTI	FUSILLI MACARONI PAPPARDELLE TAGLIATELLE	TUBETTINI STELLINE SMALL SHELLS DITALINI

TOP PASTA TIPS

SAUCEPANS Cook pasta in a large saucepan with lots of water. This allows the pasta to move freely so it doesn't stick together. Water flows evenly around each noodle and ensures uniform cooking.

WATER For 340 g of pasta, bring 16 cups of water to a boil. Once the pasta is added, stir often until the water returns to a boil that's vigorous enough to move the pasta around.

TIMING Most hot pasta dishes do not hold well. Have your sauce almost ready before you start cooking your pasta, and start the countdown clock the second the water returns to a boil.

SALT Adding salt to boiling pasta water brings out the noodles' natural flavour. However, if sodium is a concern, omit or reduce the salt as desired.

TEXTURE Cook pasta until al dente, or tender but firm. Properly cooked pasta has a toothsome chew. To check doneness, remove a piece from the water and let it cool slightly. If it holds its shape (and, in the case of long solid noodles such as spaghetti, has a tiny white speck in the centre), it's ready.

COOKING LIQUID Always reserve some of the pasta cooking liquid to toss with the pasta and sauce at the end. This helps the sauce coat the noodles evenly and boosts the flavour.

DRAIN Make sure to drain cooked pasta very well. Any liquid left on it will dilute your sauce.

STARCH Don't rinse cooked pasta, because the starch on the surface of each piece helps the sauce adhere. The only exceptions are pasta salad and other cold noodle dishes; for these, rinse pasta under cold water to stop the cooking process, then immediately toss with olive oil to prevent clumping.

SERVE Cooked pasta continues to cook and absorb sauce as it sits. For best results, serve it right away.

Buying & Using Asian Noodles

CHINESE WHEAT NOODLES These thin, cream-coloured noodles, called *yet ca mein*, are served in soups or stir-fries in many parts of China. You can buy them either dried in the Asian section of your grocery store or fresh in the refrigerated section near the sushi or tofu. There are similar Japanese versions of these noodles.

STEAMED CHOW MEIN NOODLES These thin, wavy yellow noodles get their colour from eggs. When shallow-fried in a wok into a crispy disc, they are the base for Cantonese chow mein. Look for fresh noodles in the refrigerated section near the sushi or tofu. If you can't find them, look for the dried variety in the Asian section of your grocery store.

RICE NOODLES Rice stick vermicelli are the threadlike rice flour–based noodles most often seen in Vietnamese cooking, in fresh rolls, cold salads and stir-fries. Thicker, wider rice stick noodles are used in stir-fries, soups and dishes such as pad Thai. Simple to prepare by either soaking or cooking, rice noodles are typically sold dried. Look for them in the Asian section of your grocery store.

SOBA NOODLES These thin dried Japanese noodles are made from buckwheat and wheat flours; there are also gluten-free versions made with all buckwheat flour. Recipes calling for buckwheat noodles can also be made with *cha soba*, which are flavoured with green tea.

SOMEN NOODLES These dried Japanese wheat noodles are often enjoyed in soups and served cold for dipping into savoury sauces. They are white and about as thin as angel hair pasta.

UDON NOODLES These thick, chewy Japanese wheat noodles come packaged in convenient 200 g pouches that are ready to use in recipes. Udon are excellent in soups or stir-fries. Similar to gnocchi, they don't need to be refrigerated until the packages are opened, and they don't take long to cook. Look for them in the Asian section of your grocery store.

SWEET POTATO VERMICELLI Also called glass noodles, these translucent Korean noodles are a key ingredient in *japchae*. They are delicious hot or at room temperature. Look for packages of the dried noodles—often labelled with their Korean name, *dang myun* (or a similar spelling)—in your local Asian market or in the Asian section of your grocery store.

Garlic Shrimp Spaghetti

HANDS-ON TIME
15 MINUTES

•

TOTAL TIME
15 MINUTES

•

MAKES
4 SERVINGS

What you need

340 g	spaghetti
¼ cup	extra-virgin olive oil
2	cloves garlic, thinly sliced
¼ tsp	hot pepper flakes
¼ tsp	salt
450 g	large shrimp (31 to 40 count), peeled and deveined
⅓ cup	dry white wine (see tip, below)
¼ cup	chopped fresh parsley

How to make it

In large saucepan of boiling salted water, cook pasta according to package instructions until al dente. Drain pasta; return to saucepan.

Meanwhile, in large skillet, heat oil over medium heat; cook garlic, hot pepper flakes and salt, stirring, just until garlic begins to turn golden, about 30 seconds. Add shrimp; cook, stirring, until pink and opaque throughout, about 3 minutes.

Add wine; increase heat to medium-high and cook until almost no liquid remains, about 2 minutes. Stir in parsley; cook for 1 minute. Add to pasta; toss to coat.

TIP FROM THE TEST KITCHEN
If you don't have wine, or don't want to use it, you can substitute sodium-reduced chicken broth mixed with 1 tbsp white wine vinegar.

NUTRITIONAL INFORMATION, PER SERVING: about 539 cal, 28 g pro, 17 g total fat (2 g sat. fat), 65 g carb, 4 g fibre, 129 mg chol, 497 mg sodium. % RDI: 6% calcium, 40% iron, 7% vit A, 10% vit C, 84% folate.

Zucchini Ribbon and Caper Pasta

HANDS-ON TIME	•	TOTAL TIME	•	MAKES
20 MINUTES		20 MINUTES		4 SERVINGS

What you need

340 g	spaghetti
4	zucchini
1 tbsp	olive oil
half	red onion, thinly sliced
1 tbsp	capers, drained and rinsed (see tip, page 33)
1	clove garlic, crushed
2 tsp	grated lemon zest
pinch	hot pepper flakes
¼ cup	grated Parmesan cheese
1 tbsp	lemon juice
pinch	each salt and pepper

How to make it

In large saucepan of boiling salted water, cook pasta according to package instructions until al dente. Reserving ⅓ cup of the cooking liquid, drain pasta.

Meanwhile, using vegetable peeler, slice zucchini lengthwise into long ribbons.

In large skillet, heat oil over medium heat; cook zucchini, red onion and capers, stirring occasionally, until onion is softened, about 5 minutes. Add garlic, lemon zest and hot pepper flakes; cook, stirring, for 1 minute.

Add pasta, Parmesan and lemon juice; toss together, adding enough of the reserved cooking liquid to coat. Sprinkle with salt and pepper.

TIP FROM THE TEST KITCHEN
To make this pasta into an easy, elegant appetizer, simply plate half-size portions.

NUTRITIONAL INFORMATION, PER SERVING: about 417 cal, 15 g pro, 7 g total fat (2 g sat. fat), 75 g carb, 7 g fibre, 5 mg chol, 421 mg sodium, 557 mg potassium. % RDI: 11% calcium, 28% iron, 19% vit A, 18% vit C, 94% folate.

Spaghetti With Amatriciana Sauce

| HANDS-ON TIME 35 MINUTES | • | TOTAL TIME 35 MINUTES | • | MAKES 4 TO 6 SERVINGS |

What you need

4	tomatoes (about 900 g)
115 g	thinly sliced guanciale (see tip, below)
2	cloves garlic, thinly sliced
¼ tsp	hot pepper flakes
6	leaves fresh basil, torn
340 g	spaghetti
⅓ cup	grated pecorino cheese

How to make it

Score an X in bottom of each tomato. In large saucepan of boiling water, cook tomatoes until skins begin to split, 20 to 30 seconds. Using slotted spoon, transfer to bowl of ice water and chill for 1 minute; drain. Using paring knife, peel off skins; seed and dice tomatoes. Set aside.

Cut guanciale into narrow strips. In large skillet, cook guanciale over medium heat until translucent and fat is rendered, about 3 minutes. Add garlic and hot pepper flakes; cook, stirring, for 1 minute.

Stir in tomatoes and any juices, and three-quarters of the basil; bring to simmer and cook, stirring occasionally, for 10 minutes.

Meanwhile, in large saucepan of boiling salted water, cook pasta according to package instructions until al dente. Reserving 1 cup of the cooking liquid, drain pasta; return to saucepan.

Stir tomato mixture into pasta, adding enough of the reserved cooking liquid to coat; cook for 1 minute. Sprinkle with pecorino and remaining basil.

TIP FROM THE TEST KITCHEN

Guanciale is Italian salt-cured bacon made from pig's jowl or cheek. If you can't find any, substitute pancetta. In a pinch, you can use regular bacon, but it will give the dish a smokier flavour.

NUTRITIONAL INFORMATION, PER EACH OF 6 SERVINGS: about 316 cal, 14 g pro, 8 g total fat (3 g sat. fat), 48 g carb, 4 g fibre, 24 mg chol, 524 mg sodium, 348 mg potassium. % RDI: 3% calcium, 18% iron, 11% vit A, 25% vit C, 58% folate.

Time-saver: Substitute four chicken cutlets for the two breasts and skip the cutting step.

Chicken and Sun-Dried Tomato Spaghettini

HANDS-ON TIME
30 MINUTES

•

TOTAL TIME
30 MINUTES

•

MAKES
4 TO 6 SERVINGS

What you need

2	boneless skinless chicken breasts
¼ tsp	each salt and pepper
4 tsp	extra-virgin olive oil
1	small red onion, thinly sliced
½ cup	thinly sliced drained oil-packed sun-dried tomatoes
2	cloves garlic, minced
1⅓ cups	sodium-reduced chicken broth
½ cup	dry white wine
2 tbsp	butter
340 g	whole wheat spaghettini or capellini
5 cups	baby spinach (about 140 g)
½ cup	crumbled soft goat cheese (chèvre)

How to make it

Place 1 chicken breast on cutting board. Holding knife blade parallel to board and with opposite hand on top of chicken, slice horizontally all the way through to form 2 thin cutlets. Repeat with remaining chicken; sprinkle cutlets with a pinch each of the salt and pepper.

In large nonstick skillet, heat 2 tsp of the oil over medium-high heat; cook chicken, turning once, until browned and no longer pink inside, about 6 minutes. Transfer to cutting board; slice thinly across the grain.

In same skillet, heat remaining oil over medium heat; cook red onion, stirring, until browned, about 5 minutes. Stir in sun-dried tomatoes and garlic; cook, stirring, for 1 minute. Stir in broth and wine; bring to boil. Reduce heat to simmer; cook for 2 minutes. Stir in butter. Return chicken and any accumulated juices to pan; stir in remaining salt and pepper.

Meanwhile, in large saucepan of boiling salted water, cook pasta according to package instructions until al dente. Reserving ½ cup of the cooking liquid, drain pasta; return to saucepan.

Stir spinach and chicken mixture into pasta, adding enough of the reserved cooking liquid to coat. Sprinkle with goat cheese.

NUTRITIONAL INFORMATION, PER EACH OF 6 SERVINGS:
about 398 cal, 24 g pro, 13 g total fat (6 g sat. fat), 49 g carb, 6 g fibre, 43 mg chol, 572 mg sodium, 515 mg potassium. % RDI: 6% calcium, 24% iron, 34% vit A, 22% vit C, 24% folate.

Creamy Chicken and Mushroom Pasta

HANDS-ON TIME 40 MINUTES	•	TOTAL TIME 40 MINUTES	•	MAKES 4 SERVINGS

What you need

340 g	boneless skinless chicken breasts
¼ tsp	each salt and pepper
2 tbsp	olive oil
340 g	cremini mushrooms, stemmed and sliced
4	sprigs fresh thyme
1 cup	sodium-reduced chicken broth
⅓ cup	whipping cream (35%)
¼ cup	chopped fresh parsley
1 tsp	Dijon mustard
340 g	whole wheat spaghetti (see tip, below)
¼ cup	grated Parmesan cheese
	coarsely ground pepper (optional)

How to make it

Sprinkle chicken with a pinch each of the salt and pepper.

In large skillet, heat 1 tbsp of the oil over medium-high heat; cook chicken, turning once, until no longer pink inside, 10 to 12 minutes. Transfer to cutting board; slice thinly across the grain.

In same skillet, heat remaining oil over medium heat; cook mushrooms, thyme and remaining salt and pepper, stirring, until mushrooms are tender and golden, about 8 minutes.

Stir in broth; bring to boil. Cook for 2 minutes. Stir in cream, parsley and mustard; reduce heat to simmer and cook, stirring occasionally, until slightly thickened, about 5 minutes. Discard thyme.

Meanwhile, in large saucepan of boiling salted water, cook pasta according to package instructions until al dente. Reserving 1 cup of the cooking liquid, drain pasta; return to saucepan.

Stir mushroom sauce and chicken into pasta, adding enough of the reserved cooking liquid to coat. Sprinkle with Parmesan and pepper (if using).

TIP FROM THE TEST KITCHEN
You can substitute any long pasta, such as bucatini, spaghettini or linguine, for the whole wheat spaghetti.

NUTRITIONAL INFORMATION, PER SERVING: about 568 cal, 38 g pro, 18 g total fat (7 g sat. fat), 68 g carb, 9 g fibre, 80 mg chol, 803 mg sodium, 778 mg potassium. % RDI: 14% calcium, 26% iron, 11% vit A, 8% vit C, 13% folate.

Cremini mushrooms are just young portobellos;
they have a similar rich flavour.

Spaghetti With Tuna, Tomatoes and Capers

HANDS-ON TIME	TOTAL TIME	MAKES
25 MINUTES	25 MINUTES	4 TO 6 SERVINGS

What you need

450 g	plum tomatoes (about 4), see tip, below
340 g	spaghetti
¼ cup	extra-virgin olive oil
¼ cup	capers, drained and rinsed (see tip, page 33)
½ cup	chopped fresh parsley
3	cloves garlic, thinly sliced
¼ tsp	each salt and hot pepper flakes
2	cans (each 170 g) water-packed solid white tuna, drained and flaked

How to make it

Score an X in bottom of each tomato. In large saucepan of boiling water, cook tomatoes until skins begin to split, 20 to 30 seconds. Using slotted spoon, transfer to bowl of ice water and chill for 1 minute; drain. Using paring knife, peel off skins; seed and dice tomatoes. Set aside.

In same saucepan, cook pasta according to package instructions until al dente. Reserving ¼ cup of the cooking liquid, drain pasta; return to saucepan.

Meanwhile, in small skillet, heat oil over medium-high heat; cook capers, stirring, for 1 minute.

Add parsley, garlic, salt and hot pepper flakes; cook, stirring, for 2 minutes. Stir into pasta; stir in tomatoes and tuna, adding enough of the reserved cooking liquid to coat.

TIP FROM THE TEST KITCHEN
Tomato season is an ideal time to make this dish for the sweetest flavour, but hothouse plum tomatoes also work well in the colder months.

NUTRITIONAL INFORMATION, PER EACH OF 6 SERVINGS:
about 360 cal, 20 g pro, 11 g total fat (2 g sat. fat), 46 g carb, 4 g fibre, 13 mg chol, 588 mg sodium, 351 mg potassium. % RDI: 3% calcium, 25% iron, 11% vit A, 25% vit C, 60% folate.

Spaghettini With Scallop Arrabbiata

HANDS-ON TIME
40 MINUTES
•
TOTAL TIME
40 MINUTES
•
MAKES
4 TO 6 SERVINGS

What you need

340 g	spaghettini
400 g	jumbo scallops (20 to 40 count), see tip, below
½ tsp	salt
2 tbsp	extra-virgin olive oil
55 g	thinly sliced pancetta, coarsely chopped
1	small onion, chopped
2	cloves garlic, minced
½ tsp	hot pepper flakes
¼ tsp	pepper
1	can (540 mL) whole tomatoes, crushed by hand
2 tbsp	chopped fresh parsley

How to make it

In large saucepan of boiling salted water, cook pasta according to package instructions until al dente. Drain pasta; return to saucepan.

Meanwhile, sprinkle scallops with ¼ tsp of the salt. In skillet, heat 1 tbsp of the oil over medium-high heat; working in batches, cook scallops, turning once, until golden, about 2 minutes. Transfer to plate; set aside.

Drain oil from skillet; wipe clean. Add remaining oil to skillet; heat over medium heat. Cook pancetta, stirring, until crisp, about 5 minutes.

Add onion, garlic, hot pepper flakes, pepper and remaining salt; cook, stirring occasionally, until onion is softened, about 5 minutes. Add tomatoes; cook, stirring occasionally and breaking up tomatoes with spoon, until thickened, about 10 minutes.

Stir in parsley and scallops; cook until scallops are opaque throughout, about 1 minute. Stir into pasta.

TIP FROM THE TEST KITCHEN
A tough little muscle runs up the side of a scallop and serves as a "foot" to anchor the mollusk in place. If it's still attached, remove it before cooking. Look for a darker or pinkish area along the edge and peel it off with your fingers.

NUTRITIONAL INFORMATION, PER EACH OF 6 SERVINGS:
about 372 cal, 20 g pro, 10 g total fat (3 g sat. fat), 49 g carb, 3 g fibre, 28 mg chol, 810 mg sodium, 465 mg potassium. % RDI: 6% calcium, 26% iron, 4% vit A, 23% vit C, 58% folate.

Mediterranean Chicken and Spinach Pasta

HANDS-ON TIME	TOTAL TIME	MAKES
35 MINUTES	35 MINUTES	4 SERVINGS

What you need

450 g	boneless skinless chicken breasts, thinly sliced
¼ tsp	each salt and pepper
2 tbsp	olive oil
half	small onion, thinly sliced
225 g	cremini mushrooms, stemmed and thinly sliced
3	cloves garlic, minced
1 tsp	dried oregano
⅓ cup	dry white wine
⅓ cup	sodium-reduced chicken broth
4 cups	packed baby spinach
340 g	spaghettini (see tip, below)
½ cup	crumbled feta cheese

How to make it

Sprinkle chicken with a pinch each of the salt and pepper. In large nonstick skillet, heat 1 tbsp of the oil over medium-high heat; cook chicken, stirring, until browned, about 4 minutes Transfer to plate; keep warm.

In same skillet, heat remaining oil over medium heat; cook onion, stirring occasionally, until softened, about 5 minutes. Add mushrooms, garlic and oregano; cook, stirring, until mushrooms are slightly softened, about 4 minutes.

Add wine and broth, scraping up browned bits from bottom of skillet. Add chicken and remaining salt and pepper; bring to simmer and cook until chicken is no longer pink inside, about 5 minutes. Stir in spinach until wilted.

Meanwhile, In large saucepan of boiling salted water, cook pasta according to package instructions until al dente. Reserving ⅓ cup of the cooking liquid, drain pasta; return to saucepan. Stir in chicken mixture, adding enough of the reserved cooking liquid to coat. Sprinkle with feta.

TIP FROM THE TEST KITCHEN
To boost the fibre content of this satisfying meal, substitute whole wheat spaghettini.

NUTRITIONAL INFORMATION, PER SERVING: about 589 cal, 42 g pro, 14 g total fat (5 g sat. fat), 70 g carb, 6 g fibre, 83 mg chol, 745 mg sodium, 839 mg potassium. % RDI: 16% calcium, 38% iron, 33% vit A, 8% vit C, 105% folate.

Bucatini With Sausage and Eggplant Sauce

HANDS-ON TIME	TOTAL TIME	MAKES
45 MINUTES	55 MINUTES	4 SERVINGS

What you need

2	large eggplants, peeled and cut in 1-inch (2.5 cm) cubes
2 tsp	salt
1 tbsp	olive oil
2	mild Italian sausages, casings removed
1	can (796 mL) whole tomatoes
¼ cup	dry red wine (optional)
¼ tsp	Italian herb seasoning or dried basil
pinch	each salt and granulated sugar
450 g	bucatini or other long pasta
	shaved Parmesan cheese (optional)
	hot pepper flakes (optional)

How to make it

In colander, toss eggplant with salt. Let stand for 10 to 30 minutes to release bitter juices. Squeeze out excess liquid and pat dry.

In Dutch oven or large heavy-bottomed saucepan, heat oil over medium-high heat; cook sausages, breaking up with spoon, just until beginning to brown. Add eggplant; cook, stirring, until eggplant is softened and sausage is no longer pink.

Add tomatoes, breaking up with spoon. Stir in wine (if using), Italian seasoning, salt and sugar; bring to boil. Reduce heat, cover and simmer, stirring occasionally, for 20 minutes.

Meanwhile, in large saucepan of boiling salted water, cook pasta according to package instructions until al dente; drain. Divide among serving plates; top with sauce. Sprinkle with Parmesan (if using) and hot pepper flakes (if using).

NUTRITIONAL INFORMATION, PER SERVING: about 697 cal, 25 g pro, 18 g total fat (5 g sat. fat), 112 g carb, 12 g fibre, 26 mg chol, 1,466 mg sodium, 863 mg potassium. % RDI: 10% calcium, 52% iron, 3% vit A, 52% vit C, 124% folate.

Spice this dish up by substituting hot
Italian sausages for the mild.

Spring Primavera Pasta With Goat Cheese

HANDS-ON TIME	•	TOTAL TIME	•	MAKES
25 MINUTES		25 MINUTES		4 SERVINGS

What you need

225 g	spelt spaghetti (see tip, below)
1	bunch (about 450 g) asparagus, trimmed and cut in 2-inch (5 cm) lengths
2 cups	sugar snap peas, trimmed
2 tsp	olive oil
4	cloves garlic, minced
¼ tsp	hot pepper flakes
pinch	each salt, pepper and nutmeg
1 cup	frozen green peas
1 tbsp	all-purpose flour
1 cup	milk
¼ cup	crumbled soft goat cheese (chèvre)
½ tsp	grated lemon zest
4 tsp	lemon juice
¼ cup	chopped fresh chives
6	leaves fresh basil, torn
2 tbsp	chopped fresh mint

How to make it

In large saucepan of boiling lightly salted water, cook pasta according to package instructions until al dente, adding asparagus and sugar snap peas during last 2 minutes of cooking. Reserving 1 cup of the cooking liquid, drain pasta mixture. Set aside.

In large nonstick skillet, heat oil over medium heat; cook garlic, hot pepper flakes, salt, pepper and nutmeg, stirring, for 1 minute. Stir in frozen peas. Sprinkle with flour; cook, stirring constantly, for 1 minute. Stir in milk and ½ cup of the reserved cooking liquid; bring to boil. Reduce heat to simmer and cook, stirring occasionally, until slightly thickened, about 5 minutes.

Stir in half of the goat cheese until melted. Stir in pasta mixture, lemon zest, lemon juice, half of the chives, the basil, mint and enough of the remaining cooking liquid to coat; cook, stirring, for 1 minute. Sprinkle with remaining goat cheese and chives.

TIP FROM THE TEST KITCHEN
Look for spelt pasta in the organic or gourmet section of your supermarket, or substitute any other whole grain pasta.

NUTRITIONAL INFORMATION, PER SERVING: about 359 cal, 16 g pro, 8 g total fat (3 g sat. fat), 58 g carb, 9 g fibre, 9 mg chol, 586 mg sodium, 487 mg potassium. % RDI: 13% calcium, 27% iron, 27% vit A, 45% vit C, 78% folate.

Spaghetti Carbonara With Prosciutto

HANDS-ON TIME	•	TOTAL TIME	•	MAKES
5 MINUTES		15 MINUTES		4 SERVINGS

What you need

340 g	spaghetti
4	eggs, lightly beaten (or 1 cup pasteurized whole eggs)
170 g	chopped prosciutto
¼ cup	grated Parmesan cheese (approx)
¼ cup	chopped fresh parsley
1 tbsp	whipping cream (35%)
¼ tsp	pepper

How to make it

In large saucepan of boiling salted water, cook pasta according to package instructions until al dente.

Meanwhile, in large bowl, whisk together eggs, prosciutto, Parmesan, parsley, cream and pepper. Set aside.

Drain pasta; immediately add to egg mixture, tossing to lightly cook eggs and coat pasta. Sprinkle with more Parmesan, if desired.

TIP FROM THE TEST KITCHEN

The key to silky carbonara sauce is to toss the pasta constantly as you add it to the egg mixture. If it stops moving—even for a second—the eggs will start to clump.

NUTRITIONAL INFORMATION, PER SERVING: about 498 cal, 27 g pro, 13 g total fat (5 g sat. fat), 65 g carb, 4 g fibre, 219 mg chol, 927 mg sodium, 291 mg potassium. % RDI: 11% calcium, 31% iron, 12% vit A, 7% vit C, 92% folate.

Don't like rapini? Try milder Broccolini instead.

Pasta With Rapini, Gorgonzola and Walnuts

HANDS-ON TIME	•	TOTAL TIME	•	MAKES
30 MINUTES		30 MINUTES		4 SERVINGS

What you need

¼ cup	extra-virgin olive oil
1	red onion, thinly sliced
½ tsp	each salt and pepper
2	cloves garlic, minced
2 tsp	red wine vinegar
1	bunch rapini
340 g	bucatini or other long pasta
85 g	Gorgonzola cheese, crumbled
1 cup	toasted chopped walnuts

How to make it

In skillet, heat half of the oil over medium-low heat; cook red onion and ¼ tsp each of the salt and pepper, stirring occasionally, until onion is tender and golden, about 15 minutes. Add garlic; cook, stirring, for 5 minutes. Stir in vinegar.

Meanwhile, trim bottom ½ inch (1 cm) from rapini stems; cut rapini in half. In large saucepan of boiling salted water, cook rapini until tender, about 2 minutes; drain. Stir into red onion mixture.

Meanwhile, in separate large saucepan of boiling salted water, cook pasta according to package instructions until al dente. Reserving ⅓ cup of the cooking liquid, drain pasta; return to saucepan.

Stir red onion mixture, Gorgonzola and remaining oil, salt and pepper into pasta, adding enough of the reserved cooked liquid to coat. Sprinkle with walnuts.

NUTRITIONAL INFORMATION, PER SERVING: about 760 cal, 23 g pro, 42 g total fat (8 g sat. fat), 78 g carb, 9 g fibre, 21 mg chol, 1,075 mg sodium, 480 mg potassium. % RDI: 25% calcium, 43% iron, 24% vit A, 20% vit C, 122% folate.

Springtime Spaghetti Alla Carbonara

HANDS-ON TIME	TOTAL TIME	MAKES
25 MINUTES	25 MINUTES	4 SERVINGS

What you need

LEMON PARSLEY BREAD CRUMBS:

4 tsp	extra-virgin olive oil
1 cup	fresh bread crumbs
1 tbsp	chopped fresh parsley
1 tsp	grated lemon zest

PASTA:

3	eggs
½ tsp	pepper
pinch	salt
340 g	spaghetti
1	bunch asparagus (about 450 g), shaved into ribbons (see tip, below)
¼ cup	grated Parmesan cheese
1 tbsp	lemon juice

How to make it

LEMON PARSLEY BREAD CRUMBS: In skillet, heat oil over medium-high heat; cook bread crumbs, parsley and lemon zest, stirring often, until crisp and golden, about 5 minutes. Transfer to bowl; set aside.

PASTA: In large bowl, beat together eggs, pepper and salt; set aside. In large saucepan of boiling salted water, cook pasta according to package instructions until al dente, adding asparagus during last 1 minute of cooking. Reserving 1 cup of the cooking liquid, drain pasta mixture.

Immediately add pasta mixture to egg mixture; toss together, adding enough of the reserved cooking liquid to coat pasta and make sauce creamy.

Stir in Parmesan and lemon juice. Divide among serving plates; sprinkle with Lemon Parsley Bread Crumbs.

TIP FROM THE TEST KITCHEN
To make asparagus ribbons, gently run a vegetable peeler down the length of asparagus spears to peel into thin strips.

NUTRITIONAL INFORMATION, PER SERVING: about 527 cal, 23 g pro, 13 g total fat (3 g sat. fat), 80 g carb, 5 g fibre, 143 mg chol, 787 mg sodium, 353 mg potassium. % RDI: 12% calcium, 34% iron, 17% vit A, 15% vit C, 164% folate.

Linguine With Clams

HANDS-ON TIME	TOTAL TIME	MAKES
25 MINUTES	25 MINUTES	2 SERVINGS

What you need

675 g	littleneck clams
¼ cup	dry white wine
225 g	linguine
1 tbsp	extra-virgin olive oil
2	cloves garlic, minced
¼ cup	chopped fresh parsley
pinch	each salt and hot pepper flakes
1 tbsp	butter

How to make it

Scrub clams; discard any that do not close when tapped. In saucepan, combine clams and wine; bring to boil. Cover and cook until clams open, 4 to 5 minutes. Strain clams in cheesecloth-lined fine-mesh sieve set over bowl; reserve cooking liquid. Discard any clams that do not open; set clams and cooking liquid aside.

In large saucepan of boiling salted water, cook pasta according to package instructions until al dente; drain.

Meanwhile, in skillet, heat oil over medium-low heat; cook garlic, parsley, salt and hot pepper flakes, stirring occasionally, until garlic is softened but not browned, about 2 minutes.

Add reserved cooking liquid; bring to boil. Add pasta; return to boil and cook, stirring often, until about 3 tbsp liquid remains, about 2 minutes.

Add clams; toss until heated through. Add butter and toss to coat.

VARIATION

Linguine With Mussels
Substitute 450 g fresh mussels for the clams.

NUTRITIONAL INFORMATION, PER SERVING: about 588 cal, 21 g pro, 15 g total fat (5 g sat. fat), 88 g carb, 5 g fibre, 32 mg chol, 374 mg sodium. % RDI: 6% calcium, 86% iron, 15% vit A, 25% vit C, 112% folate.

Seafood Linguine

HANDS-ON TIME	•	TOTAL TIME	•	MAKES
45 MINUTES		45 MINUTES		4 TO 6 SERVINGS

What you need

1 tbsp	olive oil
1	onion, diced
1 cup	diced trimmed fennel bulb
2	cloves garlic, minced
2	bay leaves
¼ tsp	salt
1	can (796 mL) whole tomatoes
¾ cup	dry white wine
3 tbsp	tomato paste
½ tsp	each sweet paprika and Italian herb seasoning
¼ tsp	hot pepper flakes
450 g	mussels
450 g	large shrimp (31 to 40 count), peeled and deveined
450 g	linguine
2 tbsp	chopped fresh parsley

How to make it

In Dutch oven or large heavy-bottomed saucepan, heat oil over medium-high heat; cook onion, fennel, garlic, bay leaves and salt, stirring often, until onion and fennel are softened, about 5 minutes.

Add tomatoes, breaking up with spoon. Stir in wine, tomato paste, paprika, Italian seasoning and hot pepper flakes. Reduce heat to medium; cover and simmer, stirring occasionally, for 15 minutes.

Meanwhile, scrub mussels and remove any beards; discard any that do not close when tapped. Add to Dutch oven. Stir in shrimp to coat. Cover and cook, stirring occasionally, until mussels open and shrimp are pink and opaque throughout, 7 to 10 minutes. Discard bay leaves and any mussels that do not open.

Meanwhile, in large saucepan of boiling salted water, cook pasta according to package instructions until al dente; drain. Divide among serving bowls; top with mussel mixture. Sprinkle with parsley.

NUTRITIONAL INFORMATION, PER EACH OF 6 SERVINGS:
about 433 cal, 26 g pro, 5 g total fat (1 g sat. fat), 68 g carb,
6 g fibre, 93 mg chol, 612 mg sodium, 668 mg potassium.
% RDI: 10% calcium, 50% iron, 10% vit A, 45% vit C, 84% folate.

Artichoke Pesto Linguine

HANDS-ON TIME	•	TOTAL TIME	•	MAKES
15 MINUTES		15 MINUTES		4 SERVINGS

What you need

340 g	linguine
2	jars (each 170 mL) marinated artichoke hearts, drained and rinsed
½ cup	coarsely chopped fresh parsley
¼ cup	pine nuts, toasted (see tip, below)
¼ cup	grated Parmesan cheese
¼ cup	extra-virgin olive oil
¼ tsp	each salt and pepper

How to make it

In large saucepan of boiling salted water, cook pasta according to package instructions until al dente. Reserving ¾ cup of the cooking liquid, drain pasta; return to saucepan.

Meanwhile, in food processor, pulse together artichokes, parsley, pine nuts, Parmesan, oil, salt and pepper, scraping down side occasionally, until smooth. Transfer half to small airtight container and save for another use. *(Make-ahead: Refrigerate for up to 3 days or freeze for up to 2 weeks.)*

Stir remaining artichoke mixture into pasta, adding enough of the reserved cooking liquid to coat.

TIP FROM THE TEST KITCHEN
Toast pine nuts in a skillet over medium-low heat, stirring constantly, until they're golden and fragrant, about 4 minutes.

NUTRITIONAL INFORMATION, PER SERVING: about 454 cal, 14 g pro, 14 g total fat (2 g sat. fat), 68 g carb, 6 g fibre, 3 mg chol, 445 mg sodium. % RDI: 6% calcium, 29% iron, 4% vit A, 12% vit C, 88% folate.

Chicken Piccata Linguine

HANDS-ON TIME	•	TOTAL TIME	•	MAKES
20 MINUTES		20 MINUTES		4 SERVINGS

What you need

340 g	linguine
2	boneless skinless chicken breasts , cut in ¼-inch (5 mm) strips
2 tbsp	all-purpose flour
½ tsp	each salt and pepper
1 tbsp	each vegetable oil and butter
1	clove garlic, minced
¾ cup	sodium-reduced chicken broth
¼ cup	chopped fresh parsley
3 tbsp	lemon juice
2 tbsp	capers, drained and rinsed (see tip, below)
¼ cup	grated Romano cheese

How to make it

In large saucepan of boiling salted water, cook pasta according to package instructions until al dente. Drain pasta; return to saucepan.

Meanwhile, sprinkle chicken with flour, salt and pepper. In large nonstick skillet, heat oil and butter over medium-high heat; cook chicken and garlic, stirring occasionally, until chicken is no longer pink inside, about 5 minutes.

Stir in broth, scraping up any browned bits from bottom of skillet; bring to boil. Cook, stirring, until sauce is slightly thickened, about 2 minutes.

Stir in parsley, lemon juice and capers; stir mixture into pasta. Add Romano; toss to coat.

TIP FROM THE TEST KITCHEN
Capers are brined, so they're quite salty. We often rinse them before adding them to dishes that contain other salty ingredients to keep the sodium down.

NUTRITIONAL INFORMATION, PER SERVING: about 493 cal, 29 g pro, 11 g total fat (4 g sat. fat), 68 g carb, 4 g fibre, 53 mg chol, 888 mg sodium, 312 mg potassium. % RDI: 9% calcium, 29% iron, 7% vit A, 12% vit C, 86% folate.

Pancetta, Cherry Tomato and Basil Spaghetti

HANDS-ON TIME	•	TOTAL TIME	•	MAKES
30 MINUTES		30 MINUTES		6 SERVINGS

What you need

375 g	spaghetti or other long pasta
2 tbsp	olive oil
250 g	thinly sliced pancetta, cut in strips
2	shallots, thinly sliced
2	cloves garlic, finely chopped
¼ cup	dry red wine
¼ tsp	hot pepper flakes
3½ cups	cherry or grape tomatoes, halved
½ cup	lightly packed fresh basil, thinly sliced (see tip, below)
3 tbsp	pine nuts, toasted (see tip, page 32)
	grated Parmesan cheese (optional)

How to make it

In large saucepan of boiling salted water, cook pasta according to package instructions until al dente. Reserving ½ cup of the cooking liquid, drain pasta; return to saucepan.

Meanwhile, in nonstick skillet, heat 1 tbsp of the oil over medium-high heat; cook pancetta, stirring occasionally, until crisp, about 5 minutes. Using slotted spoon, transfer to paper towel–lined plate to drain.

Drain fat from skillet. In same skillet, heat remaining oil over medium-high heat; cook shallots, stirring often, until golden, about 3 minutes. Add garlic; cook, stirring, for 1 minute. Add wine and hot pepper flakes; cook, scraping up browned bits from bottom of skillet, until no liquid remains. Add tomatoes; cook, stirring, until skins start to crack, about 2 minutes.

Stir basil, pine nuts, tomato mixture and pancetta into pasta, adding enough of the reserved cooking liquid to coat. Sprinkle with Parmesan (if using).

TIP FROM THE TEST KITCHEN
Thin strips of herbs or greens are called chiffonade. To slice basil quickly, stack several of the leaves in a pile and slice them in one go.

NUTRITIONAL INFORMATION, PER SERVING: about 439 cal, 19 g pro, 17 g total fat (4 g sat. fat), 52 g carb, 3 g fibre, 35 mg chol, 774 mg sodium, 346 mg potassium. % RDI: 3% calcium, 21% iron, 11% vit A, 20% vit C, 71% folate.

Tagliatelle With Caponata

HANDS-ON TIME	•	TOTAL TIME	•	MAKES
25 MINUTES		25 MINUTES		6 SERVINGS

What you need

⅓ cup	olive oil
1 cup	diced eggplant
¼ tsp	salt
⅓ cup	each diced onion and celery
⅔ cup	diced zucchini
⅔ cup	canned crushed tomatoes
3 tbsp	each pine nuts and unsalted shelled pistachios
3 tbsp	pitted black olives, chopped
2 tbsp	capers, rinsed and drained
4 tsp	raisins
1	clove garlic, chopped
pinch	pepper
1 tbsp	white wine vinegar
1 tsp	granulated sugar
500 g	egg noodle tagliatelle

How to make it

In Dutch oven or large heavy-bottomed saucepan, heat half of the oil over medium-high heat; cook eggplant and a pinch of the salt, stirring, until eggplant starts to brown, 2 to 3 minutes. Using slotted spoon, transfer to plate. Set aside.

In same Dutch oven, heat remaining oil over medium-high heat; cook onion and celery, stirring, until softened, 3 to 4 minutes. Add zucchini; cook, stirring, for 2 minutes. Stir in eggplant mixture, tomatoes, pine nuts, pistachios, olives, capers, raisins, garlic, pepper and remaining salt; bring to boil. Reduce heat to simmer and cook, stirring, for 3 minutes. Stir in vinegar and sugar.

Meanwhile, in large saucepan of boiling salted water, cook pasta according to package instructions until al dente. Reserving ½ cup of the cooking liquid, drain; return pasta to saucepan.

Stir eggplant mixture into pasta, adding enough of the reserved cooking liquid to coat.

TIP FROM THE TEST KITCHEN
The chunky caponata also makes a tasty sandwich filling or topping for fish.

NUTRITIONAL INFORMATION, PER SERVING: about 517 cal, 13 g pro, 22 g total fat (3 g sat. fat), 68 g carb, 5 g fibre, 68 mg chol, 682 mg sodium, 328 mg potassium. % RDI: 5% calcium, 36% iron, 5% vit A, 8% vit C, 113% folate.

Tagliatelle With Lemon, Shrimp and Arugula

HANDS-ON TIME	TOTAL TIME	MAKES
15 MINUTES	15 MINUTES	4 SERVINGS

What you need

340 g	egg noodle tagliatelle
¼ cup	extra-virgin olive oil
450 g	large shrimp (31 to 40 count), peeled and deveined
2	cloves garlic, chopped
1 tsp	fennel seeds, crushed
1 tsp	grated lemon zest
¼ tsp	each salt and pepper
6 cups	packed baby arugula (see tip, below)
2 tbsp	lemon juice

How to make it

In large saucepan of boiling salted water, cook pasta according to package instructions until al dente. Reserving ½ cup of the cooking liquid, drain pasta.

Meanwhile, in large nonstick skillet, heat oil over medium-high heat; cook shrimp, garlic, fennel seeds, lemon zest, salt and pepper, stirring occasionally, until shrimp are pink and opaque throughout, about 5 minutes.

Add arugula, lemon juice, pasta and half of the reserved cooking liquid; toss to coat. If necessary, gradually stir in remaining cooking liquid to reach desired consistency.

TIP FROM THE TEST KITCHEN
Baby arugula leaves are a time-saving ingredient because their young, tender stems don't have to be trimmed off.

NUTRITIONAL INFORMATION, PER SERVING: about 560 cal, 31 g pro, 19 g total fat (3 g sat. fat), 66 g carb, 7 g fibre, 210 mg chol, 741 mg sodium, 557 mg potassium. % RDI: 20% calcium, 54% iron, 23% vit A, 23% vit C, 100% folate.

Pappardelle With Creamy Chicken Sauce

HANDS-ON TIME	•	**TOTAL TIME**	•	**MAKES**
25 MINUTES		25 MINUTES		4 SERVINGS

What you need

1	pkg (250 g) pappardelle nests (see tip, below)
2	boneless skinless chicken breasts
2 tbsp	all-purpose flour
½ tsp	each salt and pepper
½ tsp	ground coriander
2 tbsp	vegetable oil
3	green onions (light parts only), sliced
1	clove garlic, minced
½ cup	sodium-reduced chicken broth
1 cup	frozen green peas
½ cup	light sour cream
2 tbsp	chopped fresh dill (or 2 tsp dried dillweed)
2 tsp	lemon juice

How to make it

In large saucepan of boiling salted water, cook pasta according to package instructions until al dente. Drain pasta; return to saucepan.

Meanwhile, place 1 chicken breast on cutting board. Holding knife blade parallel to board and with opposite hand on top of chicken, slice horizontally all the way through breast to make 2 thin cutlets; repeat with remaining chicken. Cut chicken into ½-inch (1 cm) thick strips. Sprinkle with flour, salt, pepper and coriander.

In large nonstick skillet, heat oil over medium-high heat; cook chicken, green onions and garlic until chicken is no longer pink inside, about 5 minutes.

Stir in broth and peas; bring to boil. Whisk in sour cream and dill; reduce heat to simmer and cook until slightly thickened, about 2 minutes. Stir into pasta. Add lemon juice; toss to coat.

TIP FROM THE TEST KITCHEN
Pappardelle are very broad noodles that are a good match for chunky, hearty sauces. If you can't find the dried nests, substitute narrower tagliatelle.

NUTRITIONAL INFORMATION, PER SERVING: about 448 cal, 28 g pro, 11 g total fat (2 g sat. fat), 59 g carb, 5 g fibre, 43 mg chol, 614 mg sodium, 404 mg potassium. % RDI: 9% calcium, 26% iron, 9% vit A, 10% vit C, 73% folate.

Penne With Smoked Trout and Asparagus

HANDS-ON TIME	•	**TOTAL TIME**	•	**MAKES**
15 MINUTES		20 MINUTES		4 SERVINGS

What you need

340 g	penne
1	bunch (about 450 g) asparagus, trimmed and cut in 1-inch (2.5 cm) lengths (see tip, below)
1 cup	frozen green peas
1 cup	chopped smoked trout or salmon (about 115 g)
¼ cup	chopped fresh dill or fresh parsley
2 tbsp	extra-virgin olive oil
2 tbsp	drained prepared horseradish
¼ cup	light sour cream or ricotta cheese

How to make it

In large saucepan of boiling salted water, cook pasta according to package instructions until al dente, adding asparagus and peas during last 2 minutes of cooking. Reserving 1 cup of the cooking liquid, drain pasta mixture; return to saucepan.

Stir trout, dill, oil and horseradish into pasta, adding enough of the reserved cooking liquid to coat. Divide among serving plates; top with sour cream.

TIP FROM THE TEST KITCHEN
Asparagus gets woody at the bottom of the stalk. Trim or snap off the ends and save them for making vegetable stock.

NUTRITIONAL INFORMATION, PER SERVING: about 544 cal, 31 g pro, 13 g total fat (3 g sat. fat), 74 g carb, 6 g fibre, 47 mg chol, 1,772 mg sodium. % RDI: 7% calcium, 24% iron, 14% vit A, 23% vit C, 120% folate.

Spinach, Tomato and Portobello Pasta

HANDS-ON TIME	•	TOTAL TIME	•	MAKES
25 MINUTES		25 MINUTES		4 SERVINGS

What you need

How to make it

340 g	kamut or whole wheat penne (see tip, below)
3 tbsp	pine nuts, toasted (see tip, page 32)
3 tbsp	olive oil
1	shallot, diced
3	cloves garlic, minced
2	large portobello mushrooms, stemmed and thinly sliced
2 cups	grape tomatoes, halved
6 cups	lightly packed baby spinach
2 tbsp	red wine vinegar
½ tsp	each salt and pepper
½ cup	grated Parmesan cheese

In large saucepan of boiling salted water, cook pasta according to package instructions until al dente. Reserving ½ cup of the cooking liquid, drain pasta; return to saucepan.

Meanwhile, in large skillet, heat oil over medium heat; cook shallot and garlic, stirring occasionally, until slightly golden, 3 to 4 minutes.

Add mushrooms; cook, stirring, until beginning to soften, about 4 minutes. Add tomatoes; cook over medium-high heat, stirring, until skins begin to crack, 1 to 2 minutes.

Stir mushroom mixture, spinach, vinegar, salt, pepper, pine nuts and ¼ cup of the reserved cooking liquid into pasta. If necessary, gradually stir in remaining cooking liquid to reach desired consistency. Sprinkle with Parmesan.

TIP FROM THE TEST KITCHEN
Kamut is an ancient variety of wheat. You'll find pasta made from kamut flour in the organic or natural foods aisle.

NUTRITIONAL INFORMATION, PER SERVING: about 520 cal, 21 g pro, 20 g total fat (4 g sat. fat), 72 g carb, 9 g fibre, 11 mg chol, 783 mg sodium, 712 mg potassium. % RDI: 23% calcium, 37% iron, 52% vit A, 20% vit C, 41% folate.

Make it gluten-free:
Substitute pasta made from
brown rice, quinoa or other
gluten-free grains.

Drizzle each serving with aged balsamic vinegar to add a sweet-tart edge.

Penne in Parmesan Cream Sauce With Prosciutto and Peas

HANDS-ON TIME 10 MINUTES	•	**TOTAL TIME** 15 MINUTES	•	**MAKES** 6 SERVINGS

What you need

500 g	penne
1⅔ cups	whipping cream (35%)
½ cup	grated Parmesan cheese
140 g	prosciutto, sliced
1 cup	frozen green peas
¼ tsp	each salt and pepper

How to make it

In large saucepan of boiling salted water, cook pasta according to package instructions until al dente. Drain pasta; return to saucepan.

Meanwhile, in large nonstick skillet, heat cream over medium heat until steaming. Add Parmesan, cook, stirring, until sauce is thickened, about 5 minutes.

Stir in prosciutto and peas; cook for 1 minute. Sprinkle with salt and pepper. Stir into pasta.

NUTRITIONAL INFORMATION, PER SERVING: about 641 cal, 23 g pro, 30 g total fat (17 g sat. fat), 68 g carb, 3 g fibre, 117 mg chol, 1,078 mg sodium, 319 mg potassium. % RDI: 15% calcium, 24% iron, 27% vit A, 3% vit C, 93% folate.

Grilled Sausage, Pepper and Bocconcini Pasta Salad

HANDS-ON TIME	TOTAL TIME	MAKES
35 MINUTES	35 MINUTES	4 SERVINGS

What you need

225 g	penne
¼ cup	extra-virgin olive oil
3 tbsp	red wine vinegar
1	large clove garlic, minced
¼ tsp	each salt and pepper
4	hot or mild Italian sausages
1	each sweet red, yellow and green pepper
1	head radicchio
1	tub (200 g) mini bocconcini cheese, drained and halved
¼ cup	loosely packed fresh basil, thinly sliced

How to make it

In large saucepan of boiling salted water, cook pasta according to package instructions until al dente; drain pasta. Set aside.

Meanwhile, in large bowl, whisk together oil, vinegar, garlic, salt and pepper. Set aside.

Place sausages and sweet peppers on greased grill over medium heat; close lid and grill, turning often, until juices run clear when sausages are pierced and peppers are charred all over, 10 to 15 minutes.

Slice sausages; set aside. Peel, quarter and seed sweet peppers; slice and add to oil mixture. Toss to coat.

Cut radicchio in half lengthwise; remove core. Place on greased grill over medium heat; close lid and grill, turning often, until leaves are tender and slightly charred, about 5 minutes. Transfer to cutting board; slice. Add radicchio, pasta, sausage, bocconcini and basil to sweet pepper mixture; toss to combine.

NUTRITIONAL INFORMATION, PER SERVING: about 726 cal, 35 g pro, 40 g total fat (14 g sat. fat), 57 g carb, 5 g fibre, 81 mg chol, 1,166 mg sodium, 508 mg potassium. % RDI: 32% calcium, 31% iron, 23% vit A, 197% vit C, 76% folate.

Mixed Pepper and Feta Pasta

HANDS-ON TIME	•	TOTAL TIME	•	MAKES
35 MINUTES		35 MINUTES		4 TO 6 SERVINGS

What you need

¼ cup	extra-virgin olive oil
2	sweet red peppers, chopped
1	each sweet orange and yellow pepper (see tip, below), chopped
1	onion, chopped
1	tomato, chopped
½ cup	stuffed green olives, halved
3	cloves garlic, thinly sliced
1	sprig fresh rosemary
¼ tsp	each salt and pepper
⅓ cup	chopped fresh oregano
4	slices Genoa salami or other mild salami, halved and cut crosswise in thin strips
425 g	whole wheat penne
½ cup	crumbled feta cheese

How to make it

In Dutch oven or large heavy-bottomed saucepan, heat 2 tbsp of the oil over medium-high heat; cook sweet peppers and onion, stirring occasionally, until softened, about 8 minutes.

Stir in tomato, olives, garlic, rosemary, salt and pepper; cover and cook, stirring occasionally, until sweet peppers tender, about 8 minutes.

Add oregano, salami and remaining oil; cook, stirring occasionally, for 4 minutes. Discard rosemary.

Meanwhile, in large saucepan of boiling salted water, cook pasta according to package instructions until al dente. Reserving ½ cup of the cooking liquid, drain pasta.

Stir pasta into sweet pepper mixture, adding enough of the reserved cooking liquid to coat. Divide among serving bowls; sprinkle with feta.

TIP FROM THE TEST KITCHEN
Sweet red, orange and yellow peppers taste the same, so use whatever combination of colours you like.

NUTRITIONAL INFORMATION, PER EACH OF 6 SERVINGS:
about 488 cal, 17 g pro, 16 g total fat (4 g sat. fat), 76 g carb, 11 g fibre, 16 mg chol, 773 mg sodium, 382 mg potassium. % RDI: 13% calcium, 29% iron, 23% vit A, 215% vit C, 18% folate.

Lemony Penne With Chicken and Artichokes

HANDS-ON TIME
20 MINUTES

•

TOTAL TIME
20 MINUTES

•

MAKES
4 SERVINGS

What you need

340 g	penne
2 tsp	olive oil
3	shallots, chopped
450 g	boneless skinless chicken breasts, chopped
3	cloves garlic, minced
1 tsp	Italian herb seasoning
¼ tsp	each salt and pepper
2	jars (each 170 mL) marinated artichoke hearts, drained and chopped (see tip, below)
1 tsp	grated lemon zest
¼ cup	lemon juice
½ cup	grated Parmesan cheese
¼ cup	chopped fresh basil

How to make it

In large saucepan of boiling salted water, cook pasta according to package instructions until al dente. Reserving ½ cup of the cooking liquid, drain pasta.

Meanwhile, in large nonstick skillet, heat oil over medium heat; cook shallots, stirring, until softened, about 3 minutes.

Add chicken, garlic, Italian seasoning, salt and pepper; cook, stirring occasionally, until chicken is no longer pink inside, about 4 minutes.

Stir in artichokes; cook until heated through, about 2 minutes. Stir in pasta, adding enough of the reserved cooking liquid to coat. Stir in lemon zest, lemon juice and Parmesan. Sprinkle with basil.

TIP FROM THE TEST KITCHEN
We use marinated artichoke hearts in this pasta because they have more flavour than those canned in water. Drain them well to keep the marinade from making your sauce oily and overly salty.

NUTRITIONAL INFORMATION, PER SERVING: about 537 cal, 31 g pro, 13 g total fat (4 g sat. fat), 74 g carb, 8 g fibre, 44 mg chol, 694 mg sodium, 526 mg potassium. % RDI: 18% calcium, 33% iron, 5% vit A, 25 % vit C, 96% folate.

Serve slices of leftover dry-cured chorizo with bread and olives as an easy starter.

Chorizo and Asparagus Pasta

HANDS-ON TIME	•	TOTAL TIME	•	MAKES
15 MINUTES		15 MINUTES		4 SERVINGS

What you need

340 g	rotini
1	bunch (about 450 g) asparagus, trimmed and cut in 1½-inch (4 cm) lengths
4 tsp	olive oil
3	cloves garlic, sliced
pinch	each hot pepper flakes and dried oregano
170 g	dry-cured chorizo, sliced (see tip, below)
¼ cup	grated Parmesan cheese
1 tbsp	lemon juice

How to make it

In large saucepan of boiling lightly salted water, cook pasta according to package instructions until al dente, adding asparagus during last 3 minutes of cooking. Reserving ½ cup of the cooking liquid, drain pasta mixture.

Meanwhile, in large nonstick skillet, heat oil over medium heat; cook garlic, hot pepper flakes and oregano, stirring, until garlic is light golden, about 1 minute. Add chorizo; cook, stirring occasionally, until crisp and lightly browned, about 5 minutes.

Stir in pasta mixture, adding enough of the reserved cooking liquid to coat. Stir in Parmesan and lemon juice.

TIP FROM THE TEST KITCHEN

Dry-cured chorizo doesn't require any cooking (though browning makes it crisp and extra savoury). If you want to substitute fresh chorizo, be sure to cook it through, until the juices run clear when pierced.

NUTRITIONAL INFORMATION, PER SERVING: about 607 cal, 27 g pro, 25 g total fat (8 g sat. fat), 69 g carb, 4 g fibre, 43 mg chol, 1,139 mg sodium, 457 mg potassium. % RDI: 11% calcium, 29% iron, 9% vit A, 12% vit C, 142% folate.

Chicken Penne With Peas and Mint

HANDS-ON TIME
10 MINUTES

TOTAL TIME
15 MINUTES

MAKES
4 SERVINGS

What you need

340 g	penne
1 cup	frozen green peas
2 cups	shredded cooked chicken
¼ cup	chopped fresh mint
¼ cup	lemon juice
3 tbsp	extra-virgin olive oil
½ tsp	pepper
¼ tsp	salt
½ cup	crumbled feta cheese

How to make it

In large saucepan of boiling salted water, cook pasta according to package instructions until al dente, adding peas during last 30 seconds of cooking.

Drain pasta mixture; transfer to large bowl. Add chicken, mint, lemon juice, oil, pepper and salt; toss to coat. Sprinkle with feta.

TIP FROM THE TEST KITCHEN
This dish is also delicious served cold as a pasta salad. Just add a little extra oil or even a touch of water to loosen it up before serving.

NUTRITIONAL INFORMATION, PER SERVING: about 583 cal, 30 g pro, 20 g total fat (6 g sat. fat), 70 g carb, 6 g fibre, 64 mg chol, 736 mg sodium, 273 mg potassium. % RDI: 12% calcium, 34% iron, 11% vit A, 10% vit C, 92% folate.

Spinach Pesto Fusilli With Ricotta

HANDS-ON TIME		TOTAL TIME		MAKES
25 MINUTES	•	25 MINUTES	•	8 SERVINGS

What you need

2	pkg (each 454 g) fusilli
2 tbsp	extra-virgin olive oil
3	cloves garlic, minced
1	pkg (284 g) fresh spinach, trimmed
2 tbsp	chopped fresh basil
1 tsp	salt
½ tsp	pepper
1 cup	ricotta cheese (see tip, below)
¾ cup	grated Parmesan cheese
2 tbsp	lemon juice
2 tbsp	pine nuts, toasted (see tip, page 32)

How to make it

In large saucepan of boiling salted water, cook pasta according to package instructions until al dente. Reserving ½ cup of the cooking liquid, drain pasta; return to saucepan.

Meanwhile, in Dutch oven or large heavy-bottomed saucepan, heat 1 tbsp of the oil over medium heat; cook garlic, stirring, until fragrant, about 30 seconds. Stir in spinach and basil; cover and cook for 2 minutes.

Uncover and cook, stirring, until no liquid remains, about 2 minutes. Transfer to food processor. Add salt, pepper and remaining oil; purée until smooth. Add reserved pasta cooking liquid; blend well.

Stir spinach mixture into pasta; add three-quarters of the ricotta, the Parmesan and lemon juice. Toss to coat. Divide among serving plates; top with remaining ricotta and the pine nuts.

TIP FROM THE TEST KITCHEN
This pasta dish doesn't call for a lot of oil, so splurge on rich full-fat ricotta cheese. It tastes better and doesn't add that many extra calories.

NUTRITIONAL INFORMATION, PER SERVING: about 547 cal, 21 g pro, 12 g total fat (4 g sat. fat), 88 g carb, 6 g fibre, 19 mg chol, 722 mg sodium, 315 mg potassium. % RDI: 17% calcium, 41% iron, 40% vit A, 8% vit C, 129% folate.

Silky Mushroom and Feta Fusilli

HANDS-ON TIME	•	TOTAL TIME	•	MAKES
30 MINUTES		30 MINUTES		4 SERVINGS

What you need

340 g	fusilli
1 tbsp	unsalted butter
3	cloves garlic, minced
1 tbsp	chopped fresh thyme
450 g	cremini mushrooms, stemmed and sliced
¼ tsp	pepper
1 tbsp	all-purpose flour
1 cup	milk
1	bunch spinach, trimmed and coarsely chopped
½ tsp	grated lemon zest
2 tsp	lemon juice
⅓ cup	crumbled feta cheese (see tip, below)

How to make it

In large saucepan of boiling salted water, cook pasta according to package instructions until al dente. Reserving ½ cup of the cooking liquid, drain pasta. Set aside.

Meanwhile, in large nonstick skillet, melt butter over medium-high heat; cook garlic and thyme, stirring, until fragrant, about 30 seconds. Add mushrooms and pepper; cook, stirring occasionally, until mushrooms are tender and golden, about 10 minutes.

Sprinkle with flour; cook, stirring constantly, for 1 minute. Stir in milk and reserved cooking liquid; bring to boil. Reduce heat to simmer and cook, stirring occasionally, until slightly thickened, about 4 minutes.

Stir in pasta, spinach, lemon zest and lemon juice; cook, stirring, just until spinach is wilted, about 2 minutes. Stir in feta.

TIP FROM THE TEST KITCHEN
You can substitute crumbled soft goat cheese for the feta, if you like. Goat cheese is less salty than feta, so taste the pasta and adjust the seasoning before serving.

NUTRITIONAL INFORMATION, PER SERVING: about 468 cal, 21 g pro, 9 g total fat (5 g sat. fat), 77 g carb, 7 g fibre, 24 mg chol, 545 mg sodium, 1,058 mg potassium. % RDI: 26% calcium, 44% iron, 87% vit A, 17% vit C, 146% folate.

If you're out of fusilli, try this dish
with rotini, gemelli or penne.

Sausage and Leek Fusilli

HANDS-ON TIME	•	TOTAL TIME	•	MAKES
25 MINUTES		25 MINUTES		4 SERVINGS

What you need

340 g	fusilli
2	mild Italian sausages (about 225 g), casings removed
2	large leeks (white and light green parts only), halved lengthwise and thinly sliced crosswise
pinch	each salt and pepper
¾ cup	sodium-reduced chicken broth
2 cups	grape or cherry tomatoes, halved
½ cup	grated Parmesan cheese
¼ cup	chopped fresh parsley

How to make it

In large saucepan of boiling salted water, cook pasta according to package instructions until al dente. Reserving ½ cup of the cooking liquid, drain pasta.

Meanwhile, in large skillet, cook sausages over medium-high heat, breaking up with spoon, until no longer pink, about 5 minutes. Using slotted spoon, transfer to bowl.

Drain all but 2 tsp fat from skillet; heat over medium heat. Cook leeks, salt and pepper, stirring often, until leeks are slightly softened, about 3 minutes. Add broth and bring to boil; reduce heat to simmer and cook, stirring, until leeks are softened but some liquid still remains, about 5 minutes.

Add tomatoes, Parmesan, parsley, pasta, reserved cooking liquid and half of the sausage; cook, stirring, until tomatoes are slightly softened, about 2 minutes. Sprinkle with remaining sausage.

TIP FROM THE TEST KITCHEN

The amount of fat in sausage varies. If yours is leaner and doesn't leave 2 tsp of fat in the skillet after it's cooked, just add enough olive oil to make 2 tsp.

NUTRITIONAL INFORMATION, PER SERVING: about 531 cal, 26 g pro, 15 g total fat (6 g sat. fat), 73 g carb, 6 g fibre, 37 mg chol, 942 mg sodium, 413 mg potassium. % RDI: 18% calcium, 36% iron, 11% vit A, 28% vit C, 93% folate.

Creamy Beef Noodles

HANDS-ON TIME
30 MINUTES • **TOTAL TIME**
30 MINUTES • **MAKES**
4 SERVINGS

What you need

1 tbsp	butter
1	onion, finely chopped
2	cloves garlic, minced
340 g	lean ground beef
⅓ cup	all-purpose flour
1 cup	sodium-reduced beef broth
1	can (370 mL) evaporated milk
1 cup	frozen green peas
1 cup	shredded extra-old Cheddar cheese
⅓ cup	chopped fresh parsley
4 tsp	Dijon mustard
¼ tsp	each salt and pepper
1¾ cups	elbow macaroni

How to make it

In Dutch oven or large heavy-bottomed saucepan, melt butter over medium-high heat; cook onion, stirring occasionally, until beginning to soften, about 2 minutes. Add garlic; cook, stirring, for 1 minute.

Add beef; cook, breaking up with spoon, until no longer pink, about 4 minutes. Stir in flour; cook, stirring, for 2 minutes.

Stir in broth and evaporated milk; bring to boil. Reduce heat to medium; stir in peas, Cheddar, parsley, mustard, salt and pepper. Cook, stirring, until peas are heated through, about 1 minute.

Meanwhile, in large saucepan of boiling salted water, cook pasta according to package instructions until al dente. Reserving ⅓ cup of the cooking liquid, drain pasta. Stir pasta into beef mixture, adding enough of the reserved cooking liquid to coat.

NUTRITIONAL INFORMATION, PER SERVING: about 663 cal, 41 g pro, 27 g total fat (14 g sat. fat), 62 g carb, 5 g fibre, 96 mg chol, 897 mg sodium, 737 mg potassium. % RDI: 48% calcium, 36% iron, 27% vit A, 72% vit C, 73% folate.

Evaporated milk lends creaminess to this dish without adding a lot of fat.

Swiss Chard Pasta

HANDS-ON TIME	•	TOTAL TIME	•	MAKES
20 MINUTES		20 MINUTES		4 SERVINGS

What you need | How to make it

1	bunch Swiss chard (about 300 g), see tip, below
340 g	fusilli
3 tbsp	olive oil
4	cloves garlic, thinly sliced
¼ tsp	salt
pinch	hot pepper flakes
⅓ cup	shaved Parmesan cheese

Separate leaves and stems of Swiss chard. Chop stems into about ½-inch (1 cm) pieces; coarsely chop leaves. Set stems and leaves aside separately.

In large saucepan of boiling salted water, cook pasta according to package instructions until al dente, adding Swiss chard leaves during last 2 minutes of cooking. Reserving 1 cup of the cooking liquid, drain pasta mixture.

Meanwhile, in large skillet, heat oil over medium heat; cook garlic just until beginning to turn golden, about 2 minutes. Add Swiss chard stems, salt and hot pepper flakes; cook, stirring, until stems are tender-crisp, about 4 minutes.

Stir in pasta mixture, adding enough of the reserved cooking liquid to coat. Cook, stirring, for 2 minutes; sprinkle with Parmesan.

TIP FROM THE TEST KITCHEN
This pasta is even more beautiful made with rainbow Swiss chard.

NUTRITIONAL INFORMATION, PER SERVING: about 448 cal, 15 g pro, 14 g total fat (3 g sat. fat), 67 g carb, 5 g fibre, 5 mg chol, 794 mg sodium, 348 mg potassium. % RDI: 12% calcium, 32% iron, 23% vit A, 35% vit C, 83% folate.

Italian Stove-top Mac and Cheese

HANDS-ON TIME	•	TOTAL TIME	•	MAKES
25 MINUTES		25 MINUTES		4 SERVINGS

What you need

1	plum tomato, diced
2 tsp	prepared pesto (see tip, below)
2 tbsp	butter
half	onion, finely diced
2	cloves garlic, minced
¾ tsp	Italian herb seasoning
3 tbsp	all-purpose flour
2 cups	milk
2 tsp	Dijon mustard
¼ tsp	salt
1 cup	shredded old Cheddar cheese
2½ cups	elbow macaroni
¼ cup	grated Parmesan cheese

How to make it

In small bowl, stir tomato with pesto; set aside.

In Dutch oven or large heavy-bottomed saucepan, melt butter over medium heat; cook onion, garlic and Italian seasoning, stirring occasionally, until onion is softened, 3 to 4 minutes.

Sprinkle with flour; cook, stirring, for 2 minutes. Gradually whisk in milk, mustard and salt; cook, whisking, until thickened, 4 to 5 minutes. Stir in Cheddar until smooth.

Meanwhile, in large saucepan of boiling salted water, cook pasta according to package instructions until al dente; drain pasta and return to saucepan. Add sauce; stir to coat.

Divide among serving plates; top with pesto mixture and Parmesan.

TIP FROM THE TEST KITCHEN
Store-bought pesto works well in this recipe, but for even better flavour, use any of our homemade pestos (pages 106 and 107) instead.

NUTRITIONAL INFORMATION, PER SERVING: about 612 cal, 25 g pro, 22 g total fat (13 g sat. fat), 77 g carb, 5 g fibre, 60 mg chol, 782 mg sodium, 369 mg potassium. % RDI: 41% calcium, 28% iron, 21% vit A, 3% vit C, 90% folate.

Creamy Shells With Ham and Peas

HANDS-ON TIME	**TOTAL TIME**	**MAKES**
15 MINUTES	15 MINUTES	4 SERVINGS

What you need

340 g	small shell pasta
2 tsp	olive oil
1	small onion, finely chopped
2	cloves garlic, minced
150 g	cooked boneless ham, cut in ⅓-inch (8 mm) cubes
1 cup	frozen green peas
4	eggs
¼ cup	whipping cream (35%)
3 tbsp	grated Parmesan cheese
¼ tsp	.pepper
1	green onion, thinly sliced

How to make it

In large saucepan of boiling lightly salted water, cook pasta according to package instructions until al dente; drain pasta.

Meanwhile, in large skillet, heat oil over medium heat; cook onion and garlic, stirring, until onion is softened, about 5 minutes. Add ham and peas; cook, stirring, until heated through, about 3 minutes.

Meanwhile, in bowl, whisk together eggs, cream, Parmesan and pepper. Set aside.

Remove skillet from heat; immediately stir in pasta and egg mixture until well combined. Return to low heat; cook, stirring constantly, until sauce is slightly thickened and creamy, about 2 minutes. Sprinkle with green onion.

NUTRITIONAL INFORMATION, PER SERVING: about 581 cal, 31 g pro, 18 g total fat (7 g sat. fat), 72 g carb, 4 g fibre, 227 mg chol, 931 mg sodium, 362 mg potassium. % RDI: 11% calcium, 31% iron, 22% vit A, 8% vit C, 10% folate.

Orecchiette pasta is a little thicker, but makes a good substitute for the shells.

Zucchini and Ricotta Shells

HANDS-ON TIME
20 MINUTES

•

TOTAL TIME
20 MINUTES

•

MAKES
4 SERVINGS

What you need

4 cups	medium or large shell pasta
2	zucchini (see tip, below)
1 tbsp	olive oil
½ cup	ricotta cheese
1 tsp	grated lemon zest
½ tsp	salt
¼ tsp	pepper
2 tbsp	thinly sliced fresh mint
2 tbsp	thinly sliced green onion (green part only)
2 tbsp	lemon juice

How to make it

In large saucepan of boiling salted water, cook pasta according to package instructions until al dente. Reserving ½ cup of the cooking liquid, drain pasta.

Meanwhile, quarter each zucchini lengthwise. Trim away seeds; discard. Cut flesh diagonally into slices.

In skillet, heat oil over medium-high heat; cook zucchini, stirring often, until tender, about 5 minutes.

In large bowl, toss together pasta, ricotta, lemon zest, salt, pepper and half of the reserved cooking liquid. Stir zucchini into pasta mixture; stir in mint, green onion and lemon juice, adding enough of the remaining cooking liquid to coat.

TIP FROM THE TEST KITCHEN
Green zucchini is easy to find, but this pasta is just as tasty made with yellow zucchini, if you have it.

NUTRITIONAL INFORMATION, PER SERVING: about 404 cal, 14 g pro, 9 g total fat (3 g sat. fat), 66 g carb, 5 g fibre, 16 mg chol, 580 mg sodium, 282 mg potassium. % RDI: 9% calcium, 26% iron, 12% vit A, 12% vit C, 84% folate.

Mediterranean Orzo Salad

HANDS-ON TIME	•	TOTAL TIME	•	MAKES
15 MINUTES		20 MINUTES		6 TO 8 SERVINGS

What you need

2 cups	orzo
¼ cup	each lemon juice and extra-virgin olive oil
1 tsp	liquid honey
½ tsp	each salt and pepper
pinch	dried oregano
1	sweet red pepper, diced
1 cup	diced seeded English cucumber
¾ cup	crumbled feta cheese
⅓ cup	chopped pitted Kalamata olives (see tip, below)
⅓ cup	chopped drained oil-packed sun-dried tomatoes
¼ cup	chopped fresh parsley
¼ cup	diced red onion

How to make it

In large saucepan of boiling lightly salted water, cook pasta according to package instructions until al dente. Drain and rinse under cold water.

In large bowl, whisk together lemon juice, oil, honey, salt, pepper and oregano. Add pasta, red pepper, cucumber, feta, olives, tomatoes, parsley and red onion; stir to combine. *(Make-ahead: Cover and refrigerate for up to 24 hours.)*

TIP FROM THE TEST KITCHEN
To pit several olives at once, place them on a cutting board and lightly crush with the bottom of a small saucepan to expose pits before removing.

NUTRITIONAL INFORMATION, PER EACH OF 8 SERVINGS:
about 286 cal, 8 g pro, 12 g total fat (3 g sat. fat), 37 g carb, 3 g fibre, 13 mg chol, 514 mg sodium, 194 mg potassium. % RDI: 8% calcium, 8% iron, 9% vit A, 63% vit C, 10% folate.

Keep a bag of frozen shrimp in the freezer so you can throw together quick meals like this.

Grilled Cajun Shrimp With Summer Vegetable Orzo

| HANDS-ON TIME 25 MINUTES | TOTAL TIME 25 MINUTES | MAKES 4 SERVINGS |

What you need

GRILLED CAJUN SHRIMP:

450 g	jumbo shrimp (21 to 24 count), peeled and deveined (see tip, below)
2	cloves garlic, minced
1 tbsp	lemon juice
1 tsp	Cajun seasoning
1 tsp	olive oil

SUMMER VEGETABLE ORZO:

1 cup	orzo
2	zucchini, cut lengthwise in ½-inch (1 cm) thick slices
1	carrot, cut lengthwise in ¼-inch (5 mm) thick slices
2	corncobs, husked
2 tbsp	olive oil
¼ cup	thinly sliced fresh basil
3 tbsp	lemon juice
½ tsp	pepper
¼ tsp	salt

How to make it

GRILLED CAJUN SHRIMP: In bowl, toss together shrimp, garlic, lemon juice, Cajun seasoning and oil; let stand for 10 minutes. Thread shrimp onto metal or soaked wooden skewers. Place on greased grill over medium-high heat; close lid and grill, turning once, until pink and opaque throughout, 4 to 5 minutes.

SUMMER VEGETABLE ORZO: While shrimp are marinating, in large saucepan of boiling salted water, cook pasta according to package instructions until al dente; drain and transfer to large bowl.

While pasta is cooking, in large bowl, toss together zucchini, carrot, corncobs and half of the oil. Place vegetables on greased grill over medium-high heat; close lid and grill, turning occasionally, until tender, 10 to 12 minutes.

Transfer vegetables to cutting board; chop zucchini and carrot into bite-size pieces. Cut kernels from corncobs. Stir into orzo; stir in remaining oil, basil, lemon juice, pepper and salt. Serve with shrimp.

TIP FROM THE TEST KITCHEN
To thaw frozen shrimp quickly, run them under cold water, breaking apart any icy clumps gently with your fingers.

NUTRITIONAL INFORMATION, PER SERVING: about 410 cal, 26 g pro, 11 g total fat (2 g sat. fat), 54 g carb, 6 g fibre, 129 mg chol, 428 mg sodium, 639 mg potassium. % RDI: 7% calcium, 26% iron, 49% vit A, 23% vit C, 49% folate.

Farfalle With Prosciutto and Olives

HANDS-ON TIME
30 MINUTES

TOTAL TIME
30 MINUTES

MAKES
4 TO 6 SERVINGS

What you need

340 g	farfalle (see tip, below)
2 tbsp	unsalted butter
115 g	thinly sliced prosciutto, chopped
10	black olives, pitted and chopped (see tip, page 63)
¼ cup	dry white wine
1 cup	bottled strained tomatoes (passata)
⅓ cup	whipping cream (35%)
¼ tsp	pepper
1 tbsp	chopped fresh oregano

How to make it

In large saucepan of boiling salted water, cook pasta according to package instructions until al dente. Reserving 1 cup of the cooking liquid, drain pasta; return to saucepan.

Meanwhile, in large skillet, melt butter over medium heat; cook prosciutto, stirring, just until beginning to crisp, about 3 minutes. Stir in olives; cook for 1 minute.

Add wine; cook, stirring occasionally and scraping up any browned bits, until no liquid remains, about 2 minutes. Stir in strained tomatoes, cream and pepper; bring to simmer. Cook, stirring occasionally, for 5 minutes.

Stir prosciutto mixture and oregano into pasta, adding enough of the reserved cooking liquid to coat. Cook over medium heat for 1 minute.

TIP FROM THE TEST KITCHEN
The name farfalle means "butterflies" in Italian. These pasta shapes are also called bowties.

NUTRITIONAL INFORMATION, PER EACH OF 6 SERVINGS:
about 353 cal, 12 g pro, 13 g total fat (6 g sat. fat), 45 g carb, 3 g fibre, 47 mg chol, 802 mg sodium, 259 mg potassium. % RDI: 4% calcium, 25% iron, 8% vit A, 2% vit C, 54% folate.

Mushrooms, Bacon and Swiss Chard With Gemelli

HANDS-ON TIME	•	TOTAL TIME	•	MAKES
30 MINUTES		30 MINUTES		6 TO 8 SERVINGS

What you need

2 tsp	olive oil
4	strips thick-cut bacon, diced
1	onion, finely chopped
2	sprigs fresh thyme
1	pkg (340 g) mixed fresh mushrooms, sliced (see tip, below)
½ tsp	each salt and pepper
½ cup	dry white wine
½ cup	sodium-reduced chicken broth
1	bunch Swiss chard, stemmed and leaves cut in thirds
¾ cup	whipping cream (35%)
4 cups	gemelli or similar pasta
1 cup	grated Parmesan cheese

How to make it

In Dutch oven or large heavy-bottomed saucepan, heat oil over medium-high heat; cook bacon, stirring, until crisp, about 4 minutes. Drain all but 1 tbsp fat from Dutch oven; cook onion and thyme over medium-high heat, stirring occasionally, until softened, about 3 minutes.

Stir in mushrooms and ¼ tsp each of the salt and pepper; cook, stirring, until mushrooms are browned and no liquid remains, about 5 minutes. Stir in wine, scraping up browned bits. Add broth and Swiss chard; cook until tender-crisp, about 4 minutes. Stir in cream and remaining salt and pepper. Discard thyme.

Meanwhile, in large saucepan of boiling salted water, cook pasta according to package instructions until al dente. Reserving ½ cup of the cooking liquid, drain pasta.

Stir pasta and ½ cup of the Parmesan into mushroom mixture, adding enough of the reserved cooking liquid to coat. Sprinkle with remaining Parmesan.

TIP FROM THE TEST KITCHEN

If you can't find packages of mixed mushrooms, buy the same weight of assorted loose mushrooms you like. Cremini, portobello, shiitake and button mushrooms are all tasty.

NUTRITIONAL INFORMATION, PER EACH OF 8 SERVINGS: about 397 cal, 15 g pro, 17 g total fat (9 g sat. fat), 45 g carb, 4 g fibre, 45 mg chol, 688 mg sodium, 449 mg potassium. % RDI: 17% calcium, 23% iron, 17% vit A, 8% vit C, 54% folate.

Sausage and Pesto Orecchiette

HANDS-ON TIME	•	TOTAL TIME	•	MAKES
20 MINUTES		20 MINUTES		4 SERVINGS

What you need

340 g	orecchiette (see tip, below)
1 tbsp	olive oil
2	mild or hot Italian sausages (about 280 g)
1	onion, chopped
3 cups	baby spinach
⅓ cup	prepared pesto (see tip, page 59)

How to make it

In large saucepan of boiling salted water, cook pasta according to package instructions until al dente. Reserving ½ cup of the cooking liquid, drain pasta.

Meanwhile, in large skillet, heat 1 tsp of the oil over medium heat; cook sausages, turning occasionally, until browned and almost cooked through, about 7 minutes. Transfer to cutting board; slice.

In same skillet, heat remaining oil over medium heat; cook onion, stirring often, until softened, about 5 minutes. Return sausages to skillet; cook, stirring often, until cooked through, about 3 minutes. Stir in spinach; cook until beginning to wilt, about 1 minute.

Stir in pasta and pesto, adding enough of the reserved cooking liquid to coat.

TIP FROM THE TEST KITCHEN
Small shells are another good choice if you don't have orecchiette.

NUTRITIONAL INFORMATION, PER SERVING: about 629 cal, 23 g pro, 28 g total fat (7 g sat. fat), 69 g carb, 4 g fibre, 38 mg chol, 671 mg sodium, 426 mg potassium. % RDI: 9% calcium, 36% iron, 27% vit A, 7% vit C, 95% folate.

Chili Mac

HANDS-ON TIME	•	TOTAL TIME	•	MAKES
40 MINUTES		40 MINUTES		8 TO 10 SERVINGS

What you need

675 g	extra-lean ground beef (see tip, below)
1 tbsp	olive oil
1	small onion, chopped
2	carrots, chopped
2	ribs celery, chopped
2	cloves garlic, minced
2 tbsp	chili powder
1 tsp	ground cumin
½ tsp	dried thyme
¼ tsp	pepper
1	can (796 mL) crushed tomatoes
1	can (796 mL) diced tomatoes
1	can (540 mL) kidney beans, drained and rinsed
3 tbsp	packed brown sugar
2 tbsp	Worcestershire sauce
4 cups	radiatore or other short pasta

How to make it

In Dutch oven or large heavy-bottomed saucepan, cook beef over medium-high heat, breaking up with spoon, until no longer pink, about 8 minutes. Scrape into bowl; set aside.

In same Dutch oven, heat oil over medium-high heat; cook onion, carrots, celery, garlic, chili powder, cumin, thyme and pepper, stirring, until carrots begin to soften, about 8 minutes.

Stir in crushed tomatoes, diced tomatoes, kidney beans, brown sugar, Worcestershire sauce and beef; bring to simmer. Reduce heat, cover and simmer, stirring occasionally, until celery is tender, about 20 minutes.

Meanwhile, in large saucepan of boiling salted water, cook pasta according to package instructions until al dente. Drain pasta; stir into tomato mixture.

TIP FROM THE TEST KITCHEN
Extra-lean ground beef keeps the fat content of this dish down. You can substitute lean or medium ground beef for it; just drain it well after browning.

NUTRITIONAL INFORMATION, PER EACH OF 10 SERVINGS:
about 355 cal, 23 g pro, 8 g total fat (3 g sat. fat), 49 g carb, 8 g fibre, 37 mg chol, 544 mg sodium, 863 mg potassium. % RDI: 9% calcium, 41% iron, 37% vit A, 35% vit C, 49% folate.

Chicken and Olive Rotini Toss

HANDS-ON TIME
15 MINUTES

•

TOTAL TIME
15 MINUTES

•

MAKES
4 SERVINGS

What you need

340 g	rotini
¼ cup	diced thick pancetta
¾ cup	sodium-reduced chicken broth
1	zucchini, chopped
¼ cup	pitted Kalamata olives, chopped
2 cups	shredded rotisserie chicken
5	leaves fresh basil, torn

How to make it

In large saucepan of boiling lightly salted water, cook pasta according to package instructions until al dente; drain pasta.

Meanwhile, in large skillet, cook pancetta over medium-high heat, stirring, until browned and crisp, about 5 minutes. Using slotted spoon, transfer to paper towel–lined plate to drain.

Drain fat from skillet; add broth and bring to boil. Reduce heat to simmer and cook until reduced by half, about 5 minutes.

Add zucchini and olives; cook over medium heat, stirring, until zucchini is slightly softened, about 2 minutes. Stir in chicken and pancetta; cook until heated through, about 1 minute. Add pasta and basil; toss to coat.

NUTRITIONAL INFORMATION, PER SERVING: about 462 cal, 29 g pro, 9 g total fat (2 g sat. fat), 66 g carb, 4 g fibre, 55 mg chol, 672 mg sodium, 303 mg potassium. % RDI: 3% calcium, 29% iron, 6% vit A, 3% vit C, 83% folate.

No rotisserie chicken?
Use sliced grilled chicken
breast or thighs.

Rigatoni With Ragù
opposite

This traditional broth-and-wine sauce doesn't contain tomato. It's a delicious alternative for people with tomato allergies.

Tagliatelle With Caponata
page 36

Rigatoni With Ragù

HANDS-ON TIME
35 MINUTES

TOTAL TIME
1½ HOURS

MAKES
8 SERVINGS

What you need

1 tbsp	olive oil
⅔ cup	each diced onion, carrot and celery
½ cup	diced leek (white and light green parts only)
2 tbsp	each chopped fresh rosemary and fresh sage
2	bay leaves
250 g	each ground veal, ground pork and ground turkey
1 cup	dry white wine
3 cups	vegetable broth
¼ tsp	each salt, pepper and nutmeg
500 g	rigatoni or other short pasta
	chopped fresh parsley (optional)
	grated Parmesan cheese (optional)

How to make it

In Dutch oven or large heavy-bottomed saucepan, heat oil over medium-high heat; cook onion, carrot, celery, leek, rosemary, sage and bay leaves, stirring, until vegetables are softened and golden, 5 to 7 minutes.

Add veal, pork and turkey; cook, breaking up with spoon, until no longer pink, about 5 minutes. Add wine; cook, stirring occasionally, until no liquid remains, about 7 minutes.

Stir in broth, salt, pepper and nutmeg; bring to boil. Reduce heat to medium-low; simmer until sauce is thickened, about 50 minutes. Discard bay leaves. *(Make-ahead: Let cool. Refrigerate in airtight container for up to 2 days or freeze for up to 2 months.)*

Meanwhile, in large saucepan of boiling salted water, cook pasta according to package instructions until al dente. Reserving ⅓ cup of the cooking liquid, drain pasta; return to saucepan.

Stir veal mixture into pasta, adding enough of the reserved cooking liquid to coat. Sprinkle with parsley (if using) and Parmesan (if using).

NUTRITIONAL INFORMATION, PER SERVING: about 461 cal, 27 g pro, 15 g total fat (5 g sat. fat), 52 g carb, 3 g fibre, 73 mg chol, 661 mg sodium, 417 mg potassium. % RDI: 4% calcium, 22% iron, 20% vit A, 3% vit C, 70% folate.

Leek and Hazelnut Ravioli

HANDS-ON TIME	•	TOTAL TIME	•	MAKES
15 MINUTES		20 MINUTES		4 SERVINGS

What you need

3	large leeks (white and light green parts only), see tip, below
1 tbsp	butter
2 tsp	olive oil
3	cloves garlic, minced
pinch	each salt and pepper
450 g	fresh cheese-filled ravioli
½ cup	crumbled soft goat cheese (chèvre)
⅓ cup	hazelnuts, chopped and toasted
1 tbsp	chopped fresh chives

How to make it

Cut leeks in half lengthwise; thinly slice crosswise to yield about 4 cups.

In Dutch oven or large heavy-bottomed saucepan, heat butter and oil over medium-high heat; cook leeks, garlic, salt and pepper, stirring occasionally, until leeks are tender and beginning to brown, about 10 minutes.

Meanwhile, in large saucepan of boiling salted water, cook pasta according to package instructions. Reserving ½ cup of the cooking liquid, drain pasta.

Gently stir pasta into leek mixture, adding enough of the reserved cooking liquid to coat. Sprinkle with goat cheese, hazelnuts and chives.

TIP FROM THE TEST KITCHEN

Leeks can be gritty. To clean them, slice as directed and then swish in a bowl of cold water. Rub to separate the layers and remove any grit. Let stand for a few minutes to allow the grit to settle on the bottom of the bowl, then pick the leeks straight out of the water without disturbing the grit. Drain well before adding the leeks to the recipe.

NUTRITIONAL INFORMATION, PER SERVING: about 559 cal, 20 g pro, 28 g total fat (9 g sat. fat), 60 g carb, 6 g fibre, 62 mg chol, 795 mg sodium, 318 mg potassium. % RDI: 25% calcium, 36% iron, 21% vit A, 17% vit C, 51% folate.

Mushroom Ravioli in Rich Herb Sauce

HANDS-ON TIME	•	TOTAL TIME	•	MAKES
25 MINUTES		30 MINUTES		4 SERVINGS

What you need

1 tbsp	olive oil
2	shallots, sliced
3	cloves garlic, minced
8 cups	sliced mixed fresh mushrooms (such as cremini, shiitake and portobello)
1 tbsp	chopped fresh thyme
¼ tsp	each salt and pepper
2 tbsp	butter
3 tbsp	all-purpose flour
2 cups	sodium-reduced beef broth
1 tbsp	10% cream
½ tsp	Worcestershire sauce
½ tsp	drained prepared horseradish
500 g	fresh mushroom-filled ravioli
1 tbsp	chopped fresh parsley (optional)

How to make it

In large skillet, heat oil over medium-high heat; cook shallots and garlic, stirring often, until fragrant, about 1 minute. Add mushrooms and thyme; cook, stirring occasionally, until mushrooms are beginning to brown and no liquid remains, 7 to 9 minutes. Sprinkle with a pinch each of the salt and pepper; scrape into bowl. Set aside.

In same skillet, melt butter over medium heat; whisk in flour. Cook, whisking constantly, for 1 minute. Slowly pour in broth, whisking constantly. Whisk in cream, Worcestershire sauce, horseradish and remaining salt and pepper. Bring to boil; reduce heat and simmer until thickened, about 5 minutes.

Meanwhile, in large saucepan of boiling salted water, cook pasta according to package instructions; drain. Add to skillet; stir in mushroom mixture and parsley (if using). Stir to coat; serve immediately.

NUTRITIONAL INFORMATION, PER SERVING: about 436 cal, 15 g pro, 19 g total fat (6 g sat. fat), 54 g carb, 6 g fibre, 48 mg chol, 909 mg sodium, 638 mg potassium. % RDI: 8% calcium, 28% iron, 7% vit A, 5% vit C, 13% folate.

Top with tangy crumbled goat
cheese or grated Romano cheese to
complement the earthy mushrooms.

Eggplant Gnocchi
With Brown Butter and Pine Nut Sauce

HANDS-ON TIME	•	TOTAL TIME	•	MAKES
25 MINUTES		1¼ HOURS		2 SERVINGS

What you need

1	large eggplant (about 450 g), peeled and cut in 2-inch (5 cm) cubes
½ tsp	salt
1	egg
¾ cup	all-purpose flour (approx)
2 tbsp	butter
2 tbsp	pine nuts
2 tbsp	minced fresh parsley
1 tbsp	lemon juice

How to make it

On parchment paper–lined rimmed baking sheet, toss eggplant with salt. Roast in 350°F (180°C) oven, stirring occasionally, until eggplant is very soft, about 40 minutes.

Transfer eggplant to food processor; purée until smooth with some chunks remaining. Add egg; pulse, scraping down side occasionally, until smooth. Scrape into bowl; stir in flour, adding up to ¼ cup more flour if necessary to make soft dough.

Turn out onto lightly floured work surface; knead just until dough holds together, adding more flour if necessary to prevent sticking. Shape into log; cut into quarters. Using palms of hands, roll each quarter into ¾-inch (2 cm) diameter rope.

Cut each rope into 1-inch (2.5 cm) lengths to make gnocchi. *(Make-ahead: Freeze on baking sheet until firm, about 2 hours; transfer to resealable freezer bags and freeze for up to 2 weeks.)*

In large saucepan of boiling salted water, cook gnocchi, stirring gently, until floating; boil for 5 minutes. Reserving ¼ cup of the cooking liquid, drain gnocchi.

Meanwhile, in large skillet, melt butter over medium heat; cook pine nuts, stirring, until lightly toasted and butter just begins to brown, about 3 minutes. Add gnocchi, parsley, lemon juice and reserved cooking liquid; toss to coat.

NUTRITIONAL INFORMATION, PER SERVING: about 488 cal, 12 g pro, 21 g total fat (9 g sat. fat), 65 g carb, 7 g fibre, 123 mg chol, 968 mg sodium, 400 mg potassium. % RDI: 4% calcium, 31% iron, 17% vit A, 13% vit C, 79% folate.

Sautéed Fiddlehead and Mushroom Gnocchi

HANDS-ON TIME	•	TOTAL TIME	•	MAKES
20 MINUTES		20 MINUTES		4 SERVINGS

What you need

2 cups	fiddleheads, trimmed and cleaned (see tip, below)
1	pkg (500 g) fresh gnocchi
3 tbsp	unsalted butter
1	shallot, thinly sliced
2	cloves garlic, minced
1 cup	sliced stemmed shiitake mushrooms
pinch	each salt and pepper
⅓ cup	grated Parmesan cheese

How to make it

In large saucepan of boiling lightly salted water, cook fiddleheads until bright green and tender-crisp, 5 to 7 minutes. Using slotted spoon, transfer to colander; rinse under cold water. Drain and set aside.

Add gnocchi to same saucepan of boiling water; cook according to package instructions. Reserving ¼ cup of the cooking liquid, drain.

Meanwhile, in large nonstick skillet, melt butter over medium heat; continue to cook, swirling pan, until lightly browned, about 3 minutes.

Add shallot and garlic; cook, stirring, until softened, about 2 minutes. Add mushrooms, salt and pepper; cook, stirring, until slightly softened, about 2 minutes.

Add fiddleheads to mushroom mixture; cook, stirring often, until tender, about 2 minutes. Add gnocchi, ¼ cup of the Parmesan and the reserved cooking liquid; toss to coat. Sprinkle with remaining Parmesan.

TIP FROM THE TEST KITCHEN

To trim and clean fiddleheads, snap off bright green tops, leaving 2 inches (5 cm) of each stem attached and discarding the remaining stems. Rub off the dry brown casings. Soak fiddleheads in cold water, changing the water several times to remove any grit or casing particles. Drain well.

NUTRITIONAL INFORMATION, PER SERVING: about 397 cal, 15 g pro, 13 g total fat (8 g sat. fat), 57 g carb, 4 g fibre, 39 mg chol, 1,111 mg sodium, 292 mg potassium. % RDI: 11% calcium, 7% iron, 29% vit A, 48% vit C, 1% folate.

Pumpkin Gnocchi
With Sage Butter Sauce

HANDS-ON TIME	•	TOTAL TIME	•	MAKES
35 MINUTES		2 HOURS		6 TO 8 SERVINGS

What you need

PUMPKIN GNOCCHI:

1	sugar pumpkin (about 1 kg) or butternut squash (about 900 g)
½ cup	grated Parmesan cheese
1	egg
1 tsp	salt
¼ tsp	nutmeg
3 cups	all-purpose flour (approx)

SAGE BUTTER SAUCE:

⅓ cup	butter
¼ cup	pine nuts
12	leaves fresh sage

How to make it

PUMPKIN GNOCCHI: Halve and seed pumpkin; prick skin all over with fork. Roast, cut side down, on rack on foil-lined rimmed baking sheet in 350°F (180°C) oven until flesh is tender, 60 to 75 minutes. Let cool. Scoop flesh into food processor; purée until smooth. *(Make-ahead: Refrigerate in airtight container for up to 2 days or freeze for up to 3 weeks.)*

Spoon 2 cups of the pumpkin purée into large bowl (save any remainder for another use). Stir in Parmesan, egg, salt and nutmeg. Stir in 2 cups of the flour. Stir in enough of the remaining flour, ¼ cup at a time, to make soft, sticky dough that pulls away from bowl but still sticks to spoon.

Turn out onto floured work surface; using floured hands, roll dough into log. Cut into quarters. Using palms of hands, roll each quarter into ¾-inch (2 cm) diameter rope. Cut each rope into ¾-inch (2 cm) lengths to make gnocchi.

Working in 2 batches, in large saucepan of boiling salted water, cook gnocchi, stirring gently, until floating, about 3 minutes per batch. Using slotted spoon, transfer gnocchi to large serving platter.

SAGE BUTTER SAUCE: While gnocchi are cooking, in large skillet, melt butter over medium heat; cook pine nuts, stirring, until lightly toasted and butter just begins to brown, about 2 minutes. Add sage; cook, stirring, until fragrant, about 30 seconds. Scrape over gnocchi; toss to coat.

NUTRITIONAL INFORMATION, PER EACH OF 8 SERVINGS: about 325 cal, 9 g pro, 14 g total fat (7 g sat. fat), 42 g carb, 3 g fibre, 49 mg chol, 710 mg sodium, 222 mg potassium. % RDI: 9% calcium, 24% iron, 129% vit A, 3% vit C, 49% folate.

Ricotta Gnocchi
With Sautéed Beets

HANDS-ON TIME	TOTAL TIME	MAKES
30 MINUTES	30 MINUTES	4 SERVINGS

What you need

RICOTTA GNOCCHI:

1	tub (475 g) extra-smooth ricotta cheese
1¾ cups	all-purpose flour
2	eggs, lightly beaten
½ cup	grated Parmesan cheese
¼ tsp	salt

SAUTÉED BEETS:

2 tbsp	olive oil
2	cloves garlic, thinly sliced
6	baby golden beets (about 2 inches/5 cm diameter), peeled, halved and thinly sliced (see tip, below)
2 cups	lightly packed chopped beet greens
⅓ cup	chopped walnuts, toasted
pinch	salt

How to make it

RICOTTA GNOCCHI: In bowl, stir together ricotta, flour, eggs, Parmesan and salt to make ragged dough. Turn out onto lightly floured work surface; divide into quarters. Working with 1 quarter at a time, using floured hands, roll dough into ¾-inch (2 cm) diameter rope; cut into ¾-inch (2 cm) lengths to make gnocchi. Transfer to floured waxed paper–lined baking sheet.

Working in batches, in large saucepan of boiling salted water, cook gnocchi until floating and no longer doughy in centre, about 3 minutes. Using slotted spoon, transfer to plate; keep warm.

SAUTÉED BEETS: In large nonstick skillet, heat oil over medium heat; cook garlic, stirring, until fragrant and light golden, about 1 minute. Stir in beets; cook, stirring occasionally, until tender-crisp, about 8 minutes. Stir in beet greens, gnocchi, walnuts and salt; cook, stirring occasionally, until greens are wilted and gnocchi are heated through, about 2 minutes.

TIP FROM THE TEST KITCHEN
If you can't find baby golden beets, substitute about three 3½-inch (9 cm) golden beets and cut them into wedges before thinly slicing.

NUTRITIONAL INFORMATION, PER SERVING: about 687 cal, 30 g pro, 40 g total fat (15 g sat. fat), 54 g carb, 5 g fibre, 132 mg chol, 1,035 mg sodium, 628 mg potassium. % RDI: 34% calcium, 36% iron, 42% vit A, 12% vit C, 80% folate.

If your beets don't come with
the greens attached, use
Swiss chard leaves instead.

Paprika Chicken With Noodles

HANDS-ON TIME	•	TOTAL TIME	•	MAKES
30 MINUTES		30 MINUTES		4 SERVINGS

What you need

2 tbsp	olive oil
450 g	boneless skinless chicken thighs, quartered
1	onion, thinly sliced
3	cloves garlic, minced
2½ cups	sliced stemmed cremini mushrooms
2 tbsp	sweet paprika
3 tbsp	all-purpose flour
2 tbsp	tomato paste
2 cups	sodium-reduced chicken broth
1 tsp	lemon juice
½ tsp	salt
pinch	pepper
1	pkg (375 g) broad egg noodles
½ cup	light sour cream
2 tbsp	chopped fresh parsley

How to make it

In large nonstick skillet, heat 1 tbsp of the oil over medium-high heat; cook chicken, turning once, until browned, 4 to 5 minutes. Using slotted spoon, remove to plate.

Drain fat from skillet. In same skillet, heat remaining oil over medium heat; cook onion, garlic, mushrooms and paprika, stirring often, until onion is softened, 1 to 2 minutes.

Add flour and tomato paste; cook, stirring, for 1 minute. Gradually stir in broth and bring to boil; reduce heat and simmer until thickened, about 1 minute. Return chicken to skillet; stir in lemon juice, salt and pepper.

Meanwhile, in large saucepan of boiling salted water, cook noodles according to package instructions. Drain noodles. Divide among serving plates; top with chicken mixture, sour cream and parsley.

NUTRITIONAL INFORMATION, PER SERVING: about 676 cal, 40 g pro, 20 g total fat (4 g sat. fat), 84 g carb, 7 g fibre, 176 mg chol, 1,159 mg sodium, 873 mg potassium. % RDI: 13% calcium, 52% iron, 23% vit A, 17% vit C, 135% folate.

Baked Farfalle
With Prosciutto and Mushrooms

HANDS-ON TIME	•	TOTAL TIME	•	MAKES
35 MINUTES		1¼ HOURS		8 SERVINGS

What you need

1 tbsp	extra-virgin olive oil
115 g	prosciutto, diced
1	onion, chopped
3	cloves garlic, minced
3 cups	sliced stemmed cremini mushrooms (about 225 g)
1½ tsp	dried basil
½ tsp	pepper
¼ tsp	salt
½ cup	dry white wine
1	can (796 mL) whole tomatoes
2 tbsp	tomato paste
⅓ cup	whipping cream (35%)
340 g	farfalle (see tip, page 66)
¼ cup	chopped fresh parsley
½ cup	grated Parmesan cheese

How to make it

In large skillet, heat oil over medium-high heat; cook prosciutto, stirring often, until golden, about 5 minutes.

Add onion, garlic, mushrooms, basil, pepper and salt; cook, stirring, until mushrooms are golden, about 8 minutes. Add wine; cook until almost no liquid remains, about 1 minute.

Add tomatoes, breaking up with spoon. Stir in tomato paste; bring to boil. Reduce heat to simmer; cook, stirring occasionally, for 20 minutes. Stir in cream; bring to simmer. Cook, stirring, until thickened, about 5 minutes.

Meanwhile, in large saucepan of boiling salted water, cook pasta according to package instructions until al dente. Drain pasta; return to saucepan. Stir in tomato mixture and parsley.

Transfer to 11- x 9-inch (2.5 L) baking dish; sprinkle with Parmesan. Bake in 375°F (190°C) oven until bubbly, about 30 minutes.

TIP FROM THE TEST KITCHEN
This is a good dish to make ahead and cook the next evening. Cover and refrigerate the unbaked dish for up to 24 hours; uncover and bake as directed.

NUTRITIONAL INFORMATION, PER SERVING: about 293 cal, 12 g pro, 9 g total fat (4 g sat. fat), 41 g carb, 4 g fibre, 26 mg chol, 601 mg sodium. % RDI: 12% calcium, 24% iron, 7% vit A, 28% vit C, 46% folate.

Slow Cooker Spinach and Ricotta Manicotti

HANDS-ON TIME
25 MINUTES

•

TOTAL TIME
3½ HOURS

•

MAKES
4 TO 6 SERVINGS

What you need

SPINACH AND RICOTTA FILLING:

1	pkg (300 g) frozen spinach, thawed and squeezed dry
1¼ cups	ricotta cheese
1	egg, lightly beaten
1	clove garlic, finely grated or pressed
¼ tsp	each salt and pepper

MANICOTTI:

10	tubes manicotti
1	bottle (720 mL) strained tomatoes (passata)
¼ cup	tomato paste
3 tbsp	prepared pesto (see tip, page 59)
2 tsp	onion powder
3	cloves garlic, finely grated or pressed
1 tsp	liquid honey
½ tsp	salt
¼ tsp	pepper
pinch	hot pepper flakes
½ cup	shredded mozzarella cheese
3 tbsp	chopped fresh basil

How to make it

SPINACH AND RICOTTA FILLING: In bowl, stir together spinach, ricotta, egg, garlic, salt and pepper. Spoon into piping bag fitted with large plain tip.

MANICOTTI: Pipe Spinach and Ricotta Filling into manicotti tubes to fill. In slow cooker, stir together strained tomatoes, tomato paste, pesto, onion powder, garlic, honey, salt, pepper, hot pepper flakes and 1 cup water. Place manicotti tubes in single layer in slow cooker, pressing to submerge. Cover and cook on low for 3 hours.

Sprinkle with mozzarella; cover and cook on high until melted, about 5 minutes. Sprinkle with basil.

NUTRITIONAL INFORMATION, PER EACH OF 6 SERVINGS:
about 332 cal, 15 g pro, 14 g total fat (7 g sat. fat), 36 g carb, 3 g fibre, 65 mg chol, 731 mg sodium, 577 mg potassium. % RDI: 23% calcium, 33% iron, 53% vit A, 10% vit C, 58% folate.

Greek-Style Macaroni and Cheese

HANDS-ON TIME	TOTAL TIME	MAKES
30 MINUTES	1 HOUR	6 TO 8 SERVINGS

What you need

450 g	fresh spinach, trimmed
⅓ cup	butter, melted
1	onion, finely chopped
2	cloves garlic, minced
2 tbsp	chopped fresh oregano (or 2 tsp dried oregano)
¼ cup	all-purpose flour
4 tsp	Dijon mustard
4 cups	milk
¼ tsp	each salt and pepper
¼ tsp	nutmeg
2 cups	shredded provolone cheese
1¼ cups	crumbled feta cheese
1 cup	grated Romano cheese
4 cups	Scoobi doo pasta
1½ cups	fresh bread crumbs

How to make it

In large saucepan, heat 2 tbsp water over medium-high heat; cook spinach, stirring once, until wilted, about 3 minutes. Transfer to colander to drain, squeezing out excess liquid. Chop spinach. Set aside.

In Dutch oven or large heavy-bottomed saucepan, melt ¼ cup of the butter over medium heat; cook onion, stirring occasionally, until softened, about 5 minutes. Add garlic and oregano; cook, stirring, for 1 minute. Sprinkle with flour; cook, stirring, for 1 minute.

Stir in mustard. Whisk in milk until smooth; bring to simmer. Cook, stirring frequently, until thickened, about 6 minutes. Sprinkle with salt, pepper and nutmeg. Stir in provolone, ⅓ cup of the feta and the Romano until smooth.

Meanwhile, in large saucepan of boiling salted water, cook pasta until still slightly firm in centre, about 6 minutes. Reserving ½ cup of the cooking liquid, drain pasta; return to saucepan.

Stir in milk mixture, reserved cooking liquid and spinach. Scrape into greased 13- x 9-inch (3 L) baking dish. Mix bread crumbs with remaining butter; sprinkle over pasta. Top with remaining feta. Bake on rimmed baking sheet in 375°F (190°C) oven until bubbly and golden, 30 to 35 minutes.

NUTRITIONAL INFORMATION, PER EACH OF 8 SERVINGS:
about 548 cal, 27 g pro, 28 g total fat (17 g sat. fat), 49 g carb, 3 g fibre, 84 mg chol, 1,056 mg sodium, 583 mg potassium.
% RDI: 65% calcium, 33% iron, 81% vit A, 10% vit C, 89% folate.

The Ultimate Macaroni and Cheese

HANDS-ON TIME	•	TOTAL TIME	•	MAKES
25 MINUTES		1 HOUR		8 SERVINGS

What you need

MACARONI AND CHEESE:

3 cups	elbow macaroni (about 450 g)
3 tbsp	butter
3	cloves garlic, minced
1 tsp	chopped fresh thyme
⅓ cup	all-purpose flour
4 cups	milk
2 tbsp	Dijon mustard
¼ tsp	each salt, pepper and nutmeg
pinch	cayenne pepper
1½ cups	shredded Gruyère cheese
1½ cups	shredded extra-old Cheddar cheese

TOPPING:

½ cup	panko bread crumbs
¼ cup	grated Parmesan cheese
1 tbsp	butter, diced and softened

How to make it

MACARONI AND CHEESE: In large saucepan of boiling salted water, cook pasta according to package instructions until al dente. Drain pasta. Set aside.

Meanwhile, in large heavy-bottomed saucepan, melt butter over medium heat; cook garlic and thyme, stirring occasionally, until fragrant, about 2 minutes.

Whisk in flour; cook, whisking constantly, for 2 minutes. Pour in milk in slow steady stream, whisking constantly until smooth. Cook, whisking often, until thickened, about 7 minutes.

Whisk in mustard, salt, pepper, nutmeg and cayenne pepper. Stir in Gruyère and Cheddar until melted and smooth; stir in pasta. Scrape into lightly greased 12-cup (3 L) casserole dish.

TOPPING: In bowl, mix panko with Parmesan; using fingers, rub in butter until mixture resembles coarse crumbs. Sprinkle over pasta mixture.

Bake in 400°F (200°C) oven until sauce is bubbly and topping is golden, about 25 minutes. Let stand for 10 minutes before serving.

TIP FROM THE TEST KITCHEN
The sauce might seem runny at first but will thicken when baked with the starchy macaroni.

NUTRITIONAL INFORMATION, PER SERVING: about 479 cal, 23 g pro, 24 g total fat (14 g sat. fat), 43 g carb, 2 g fibre, 72 mg chol, 576 mg sodium, 262 mg potassium. % RDI: 51% calcium, 15% iron, 25% vit A, 2% vit C, 45% folate.

Choose a sweet, crisp apple, such as Cortland,
for this unique take on mac and cheese.

Macaroni and Cheese With Apple and Sausage

HANDS-ON TIME	•	TOTAL TIME	•	MAKES
40 MINUTES		1½ HOURS		8 SERVINGS

What you need

½ tsp	vegetable oil
500 g	mild Italian sausages
3⅓ cups	elbow macaroni (about 500 g)
2 tbsp	olive oil
1	large onion, chopped
2 cups	chopped cored apple (about 1 large)
⅓ cup	all-purpose flour
4 cups	milk
3 cups	shredded old Cheddar cheese
2 tsp	chopped fresh thyme (or 1 tsp dried thyme)
½ cup	panko bread crumbs
½ cup	grated Parmesan cheese

How to make it

In large nonstick skillet, heat vegetable oil over medium heat; cook sausages, turning occasionally, until no longer pink inside, about 12 minutes. Transfer to cutting board; slice. Set aside.

In large saucepan of boiling salted water, cook pasta according to package instructions until al dente; drain. Set aside.

Meanwhile, in large heavy-bottomed saucepan, heat olive oil over medium-high heat; cook onion, stirring often, until softened, about 5 minutes. Add apple; cook, stirring often, until softened, 3 to 4 minutes. Sprinkle in flour; cook, stirring, for 1 minute.

Gradually whisk in milk; bring to boil, whisking constantly. Cook, whisking, until thickened, 1 minute. Remove from heat. Add Cheddar, sausages and thyme, stirring until cheese is melted; stir in pasta. Scrape into lightly greased 12-cup (3 L) casserole dish.

Mix panko with Parmesan; sprinkle over pasta mixture. Bake in 350°F (180°C) oven until sauce is bubbly and topping is golden, about 45 minutes.

NUTRITIONAL INFORMATION, PER SERVING: about 750 cal, 36 g pro, 36 g total fat (15 g sat. fat), 71 g carb, 3 g fibre, 90 mg chol, 1,036 mg sodium, 539 mg potassium. % RDI: 50% calcium, 25% iron, 20% vit A, 7% vit C, 75% folate.

Cheese-Stuffed Shells

HANDS-ON TIME	TOTAL TIME	MAKES
1 HOUR	2 HOURS	8 SERVINGS

What you need

CHUNKY BEEF SAUCE:

2 tbsp	extra-virgin olive oil or vegetable oil
450 g	lean ground beef
2	onions, finely chopped
4	cloves garlic, minced
1½ tsp	each dried basil and dried oregano
pinch	each hot pepper flakes, salt and pepper
1	can (796 mL) whole tomatoes, puréed
1	can (398 mL) tomato sauce

FILLING:

1	pkg (300 g) frozen chopped spinach, thawed and squeezed dry
1	tub (475 g) ricotta cheese
1 cup	grated Parmesan cheese
1 cup	shredded mozzarella cheese
¼ cup	chopped fresh parsley
2	green onions, chopped
2	eggs, lightly beaten
1 tsp	dried basil
¼ tsp	each nutmeg and pepper

STUFFED SHELLS:

1	box (340 g) jumbo shell pasta
1 cup	shredded mozzarella cheese
¼ cup	grated Parmesan cheese

How to make it

CHUNKY BEEF SAUCE: In shallow Dutch oven, heat 1 tbsp of the oil over medium-high heat; cook beef, breaking up with spoon, until no longer pink, about 5 minutes. Using slotted spoon, remove to bowl.

Drain fat from Dutch oven. In same Dutch oven, heat remaining oil over medium-high heat; cook onions and garlic, stirring, for 5 minutes. Stir in basil, oregano, hot pepper flakes, salt, pepper, tomatoes and tomato sauce. Stir in beef; bring to boil. Reduce heat to simmer; cook, stirring often, until thickened, 20 to 25 minutes.

FILLING: While sauce is simmering, in bowl, stir together spinach, ricotta, Parmesan, mozzarella, parsley, green onions, eggs, basil, nutmeg and pepper. Set aside.

STUFFED SHELLS: In large saucepan of boiling salted water, cook pasta according to package instructions until al dente. Drain and rinse under cold water; drain well and place on damp tea towel.

Spread half of the sauce in 13- x 9-inch (3 L) baking dish. Spoon heaping 1 tbsp of the filling into each pasta shell. Arrange, stuffed side up, in baking dish, packing tightly. Spoon remaining sauce over top; sprinkle with mozzarella and Parmesan. *(Make-ahead: Let cool. Cover with plastic wrap and refrigerate for up to 24 hours, or overwrap with foil and freeze for up to 2 weeks. Thaw in refrigerator for 24 hours. Unwrap dish; bake as directed.)*

Cover with foil. Bake in 350°F (180°C) oven for 30 minutes. Uncover; bake until heated through, about 20 minutes.

NUTRITIONAL INFORMATION, PER SERVING: about 621 cal, 39 g pro, 30 g total fat (16 g sat. fat), 48 g carb, 5 g fibre, 146 mg chol, 1,001 mg sodium. % RDI: 52% calcium, 40% iron, 41% vit A, 38% vit C, 67% folate.

Baked Sausage and Pepper Pasta With Mozzarella and Provolone

HANDS-ON TIME	TOTAL TIME	MAKES
40 MINUTES	1¾ HOURS	6 SERVINGS

What you need

3 tbsp	olive oil
2	onions, thinly sliced
2	each sweet red and yellow peppers, thinly sliced
3	cloves garlic, minced
2	bay leaves
¼ tsp	hot pepper flakes
900 g	mild or hot Italian sausages, casings removed
4 cups	bottled strained tomatoes (passata)
10	leaves fresh basil
450 g	rigatoni
2 cups	shredded mozzarella cheese
1 cup	shredded provolone cheese

How to make it

In large Dutch oven, heat oil over medium heat; cook onions, sweet peppers, garlic, bay leaves and hot pepper flakes, stirring occasionally, until peppers are softened, about 8 minutes.

Add sausages; cook over medium-high heat, breaking up with spoon, until no longer pink, about 6 minutes. Stir in strained tomatoes and basil; reduce heat to simmer and cook, stirring occasionally, until thickened, about 20 minutes. Discard bay leaves.

Let cool for 30 minutes; divide sauce in half, reserving 1 half for another use. *(Make-ahead: Transfer to airtight containers; refrigerate for up to 2 days or freeze for up to 2 months. Thaw; reheat in saucepan over medium heat for 8 to 10 minutes.)*

Meanwhile, in large saucepan of boiling salted water, cook pasta for 3 minutes less than package instructions for al dente. Drain pasta; return to saucepan. Add remaining sausage mixture; toss to combine. Spread in 13- x 9-inch (3 L) baking dish.

Sprinkle with mozzarella and provolone; cover with foil. Bake in 375°F (190°C) oven until bubbly and cheese is melted, 25 to 30 minutes.

TIP FROM THE TEST KITCHEN

This recipe makes a double batch of sauce to give you a head start on a second dinner. Reheat the remaining sauce and use it to make another batch of this baked pasta, or toss it with your favourite long pasta and top with a generous sprinkle of grated Parmesan or Romano cheese.

NUTRITIONAL INFORMATION, PER SERVING: about 753 cal, 35 g pro, 37 g total fat (15 g sat. fat), 69 g carb, 6 g fibre, 86 mg chol, 1,191 mg sodium, 651 mg potassium. % RDI: 39% calcium, 36% iron, 27% vit A, 122% vit C, 82% folate.

Squash, Spinach and Italian Cheese Cannelloni

HANDS-ON TIME	•	TOTAL TIME	•	MAKES
1 HOUR		2¼ HOURS		8 SERVINGS

What you need

SQUASH FILLING:

1	butternut squash (about 565 g)
1	onion, quartered
2 tbsp	olive oil
¼ tsp	each salt and pepper
¾ cup	ricotta cheese
⅓ cup	grated Romano or Parmesan cheese

SPINACH FILLING:

2 tbsp	butter or olive oil
1	leek (white and light green parts only), chopped
450 g	fresh spinach, trimmed
½ tsp	each salt and pepper

BÉCHAMEL SAUCE:

2 tbsp	butter
3 tbsp	all-purpose flour
2¼ cups	milk
¼ tsp	each salt, pepper and nutmeg
2 cups	shredded Fontina cheese
¼ cup	grated Romano or Parmesan cheese
8	sheets (8 x 6 inches/20 x 15 cm) fresh lasagna
⅓ cup	pine nuts, toasted (see tip, page 32)

How to make it

SQUASH FILLING: Peel, seed and cube squash to yield 4 cups. In roasting pan, toss together squash, onion, oil, salt and pepper. Roast in 425°F (220°C) oven until tender, about 40 minutes. Let cool. In food processor, purée together squash mixture, ricotta and Romano. Set aside.

SPINACH FILLING: While squash is roasting, in large saucepan, melt butter over medium-high heat; cook leek, stirring, until softened, about 5 minutes. Stir in spinach, salt and pepper; cover and cook until spinach is wilted, about 2 minutes. Transfer to colander to drain, squeezing out excess liquid. Chop spinach. Set aside.

BÉCHAMEL SAUCE: In saucepan, melt butter over medium heat. Whisk in flour; cook, whisking, for 2 minutes. Slowly add milk, whisking constantly; bring to boil. Reduce heat to simmer; cook, whisking, until bubbly and slightly thickened, about 5 minutes. Whisk in salt, pepper and nutmeg. Remove from heat; whisk in 1½ cups of the Fontina and the Romano until smooth.

TO FINISH: In heatproof bowl, combine pasta and enough boiling water to cover; let stand until pliable, about 2 minutes. Drain and pat dry. Cut each sheet into two 6- x 4-inch (15 x 10 cm) rectangles.

Spread 1 cup of the Béchamel Sauce in 13- x 9-inch (3 L) baking dish. Spoon scant 3 tbsp of the squash filling along 1 short side of each pasta rectangle. Top with scant 2 tbsp of the spinach filling; roll up. Arrange, seam side down, in dish, packing tightly. Pour remaining Béchamel Sauce over top; sprinkle with remaining Fontina. Cover with foil. Bake in 375°F (190°C) oven for 25 minutes. Uncover and bake until bubbly and cheese is lightly browned, about 30 minutes.

Top with pine nuts; let stand for 5 minutes before serving.

NUTRITIONAL INFORMATION, PER SERVING: about 456 cal, 20 g pro, 29 g total fat (14 g sat. fat), 32 g carb, 4 g fibre, 88 mg chol, 732 mg sodium, 691 mg potassium. % RDI: 43% calcium, 26% iron, 160% vit A, 28% vit C, 62% folate.

Hint: Leftover lasagna is always better reheated after a night in the fridge. It pays to save a few slices for lunch.

The Ultimate Lasagna

HANDS-ON TIME	TOTAL TIME	MAKES
45 MINUTES	3 HOURS	12 SERVINGS

What you need

TOMATO MEAT SAUCE:

2 tbsp	olive oil
2	onions, diced
1	each carrot and rib celery, diced
4	cloves garlic, minced
2	cans (each 156 mL) tomato paste
675 g	lean ground beef
2	cans (each 796 mL) diced tomatoes
1 cup	dry red or white wine
2	bay leaves
2 tsp	dried oregano
1 tsp	salt
¾ tsp	pepper

LASAGNA:

12	lasagna noodles
1	tub (475 g) extra-smooth ricotta cheese
1 cup	grated Parmesan cheese
1	egg
½ cup	chopped fresh basil
1	clove garlic, minced
¼ tsp	each salt and pepper
4½ cups	shredded mozzarella cheese

How to make it

TOMATO MEAT SAUCE: In Dutch oven, heat oil over medium heat; cook onions, carrot, celery and garlic, stirring occasionally, until softened, about 5 minutes. Stir in tomato paste. Add beef; cook, breaking up with spoon, until no longer pink, about 5 minutes. Add tomatoes, wine, bay leaves, oregano, salt and pepper; reduce heat to simmer and cook, stirring occasionally, until slightly thickened, about 40 minutes. Discard bay leaves. *(Make-ahead: Let cool for 30 minutes. Refrigerate in airtight container for up to 3 days.)*

LASAGNA: While sauce is simmering, in large saucepan of boiling salted water, cook noodles for 2 minutes less than package instructions for al dente. Drain; lay noodles, without touching, in single layer on tea towel.

In bowl, stir together ricotta, Parmesan, egg, basil, garlic, salt and pepper. Set aside.

Remove 1½ cups of the Tomato Meat Sauce to small bowl; set aside. In 13- x 9-inch (3 L) baking dish, spread one-third of the remaining meat sauce. Arrange 3 of the noodles over top; sprinkle with 1½ cups of the mozzarella. Top with half of the remaining meat sauce, 3 of the remaining noodles, the ricotta mixture, 3 of the remaining noodles, remaining meat sauce, then remaining noodles. Top with reserved meat sauce; sprinkle with remaining mozzarella. *(Make-ahead: Cover with plastic wrap and refrigerate for up to 3 days. Unwrap and bake as directed.)*

Cover with foil. Bake in 375°F (190°C) oven for 45 minutes. Uncover; bake until cheese is golden, 15 minutes. Cover loosely with foil; let stand for 30 minutes before serving.

NUTRITIONAL INFORMATION, PER SERVING: about 551 cal, 35 g pro, 30 g total fat (16 g sat. fat), 36 g carb, 5 g fibre, 92 mg chol, 1,065 mg sodium, 868 mg potassium. % RDI: 47% calcium, 36% iron, 36% vit A, 43% vit C, 33% folate.

Veal and Mushroom Lasagna

HANDS-ON TIME
1 HOUR
•
TOTAL TIME
2½ HOURS
•
MAKES
12 SERVINGS

What you need

VEAL AND MUSHROOM FILLING:

1 tbsp	olive oil
2	onions, chopped
3	cloves garlic, minced
1	each carrot and rib celery, finely chopped
8 cups	sliced mixed fresh mushrooms (about 675 g)
1 tsp	each dried basil and dried oregano
¾ tsp	salt
½ tsp	pepper
675 g	lean ground veal or ground turkey
1 cup	dry white wine
¼ cup	chopped fresh parsley

BÉCHAMEL SAUCE:

⅓ cup	butter
⅔ cup	all-purpose flour
5½ cups	milk
¾ tsp	salt
½ tsp	pepper
pinch	nutmeg
⅔ cup	grated Parmesan cheese

LASAGNA:

12	lasagna noodles
4 cups	shredded provolone or mozzarella cheese
¼ cup	grated Parmesan cheese

How to make it

VEAL AND MUSHROOM FILLING: In large heavy-bottomed saucepan, heat oil over medium-high heat; cook onions, garlic, carrot, celery, mushrooms, basil, oregano, salt and pepper, stirring often, until no liquid remains, about 10 minutes. Add veal; cook, breaking up with spoon, until no longer pink, about 5 minutes. Drain fat from saucepan. Add wine and bring to boil. Reduce heat to simmer; cook until no liquid remains, about 10 minutes. Stir in parsley. Set aside.

BÉCHAMEL SAUCE: In saucepan, melt butter over medium heat; whisk in flour. Cook, whisking, for 1 minute. Whisk in milk, salt, pepper and nutmeg; cook, whisking, until boiling and thickened, about 15 minutes. Whisk in Parmesan.

LASAGNA: While Béchamel Sauce is cooking, in large saucepan of boiling salted water, cook noodles for 2 minutes less than package instructions for al dente. Drain; lay noodles, without touching, in single layer on tea towel.

In 13- x 9-inch (3 L) baking dish, spread 1 cup of the Béchamel Sauce; arrange 3 of the noodles over top. Layer one-third of the Veal and Mushroom Filling, 1 cup of the Béchamel Sauce, ⅔ cup of the provolone and 3 of the remaining noodles over top; repeat layers twice. Top with remaining Béchamel Sauce and provolone, and the Parmesan. *(Make-ahead: Let cool; cover with plastic wrap and refrigerate for up to 24 hours or overwrap with foil and freeze for up to 2 weeks. Thaw in refrigerator for 48 hours. Unwrap; bake as directed, adding 15 minutes to baking time.)*

Cover with lightly greased foil. Bake in 375°F (190°C) oven for 45 minutes. Uncover; bake until golden and bubbly, about 30 minutes. Let stand for 10 minutes before serving.

NUTRITIONAL INFORMATION, PER SERVING: about 480 cal, 32 g pro, 25 g total fat (14 g sat. fat), 31 g carb, 3 g fibre, 102 mg chol, 924 mg sodium. % RDI: 49% calcium, 18% iron, 32% vit A, 5% vit C, 35% folate.

Giant Meatballs in Tomato Fennel Sauce

HANDS-ON TIME	•	TOTAL TIME	•	MAKES
1½ HOURS		1¾ HOURS		6 TO 8 SERVINGS

What you need

How to make it

TOMATO FENNEL SAUCE:

2 tbsp	olive oil
1	each onion and small carrot, chopped
4	cloves garlic, sliced
half	bulb fennel, cored and chopped
½ tsp	salt
¼ tsp	hot pepper flakes
1	can (796 mL) whole tomatoes
10	leaves fresh basil

GIANT MEATBALLS:

2 cups	cubed crustless Italian bread
1 cup	milk
1	each egg and egg yolk
450 g	each ground veal (or beef) and ground pork
2 tbsp	olive oil
½ cup	minced shallots or onion
3	cloves garlic, minced
¼ cup	chopped fresh parsley
¼ cup	grated Parmesan cheese
¼ tsp	each salt and pepper
3 tbsp	all-purpose flour

TOMATO FENNEL SAUCE: In Dutch oven or large heavy-bottomed saucepan, heat oil over medium heat; cook onion, carrot, garlic, fennel, salt and hot pepper flakes, stirring occasionally, until onion is softened, about 8 minutes.

Add tomatoes, breaking up with spoon. Stir in basil and 1 cup water; bring to boil. Reduce heat, cover and simmer, stirring occasionally, for 30 minutes. Let cool slightly.

Transfer to food processor; blend until smooth. Pour into clean Dutch oven.

GIANT MEATBALLS: While sauce is simmering, in bowl, soak bread in milk until absorbed, about 10 minutes. Squeeze out as much liquid as possible.

In food processor, pulse together bread mixture, egg, egg yolk and one-quarter each of the veal and pork just until combined. Transfer to large bowl.

In large skillet, heat 1 tbsp of the oil over medium-low heat; cook shallots and garlic, stirring, until golden, 3 to 5 minutes. Add to bread mixture; add parsley, Parmesan, salt, pepper and remaining veal and pork; mix with hands just until combined. Form into 12 large meatballs; refrigerate on baking sheet for 10 minutes. Gently roll in flour.

In same skillet, heat remaining oil over medium-high heat; cook meatballs, turning often, until golden all over, about 8 minutes. Add to Tomato Fennel Sauce; cover and simmer over medium-low heat, stirring and basting occasionally, until no longer pink inside and instant-read thermometer inserted into several meatballs reads 160°F (71°C), about 20 minutes.

NUTRITIONAL INFORMATION, PER EACH OF 8 SERVINGS:
about 387 cal, 27 g pro, 23 g total fat (7 g sat. fat), 17 g carb,
2 g fibre, 133 mg chol, 542 mg sodium, 765 mg potassium. % RDI:
13% calcium, 21% iron, 20% vit A, 32% vit C, 22% folate.

Tomato Red Pepper Cream Sauce

HANDS-ON TIME
15 MINUTES
•
TOTAL TIME
15 MINUTES
•
MAKES
ABOUT 1 CUP

What you need

1 tbsp	olive oil
3	cloves garlic, minced
¼ cup	chopped drained oil-packed sun-dried tomatoes
¼ cup	chopped jarred roasted red pepper, drained
¼ tsp	hot pepper flakes
1 cup	whipping cream (35%)
2 tbsp	sliced fresh basil

How to make it

In saucepan, heat oil over medium heat; cook garlic, stirring, until light golden, about 1 minute. Add tomatoes, red pepper and hot pepper flakes; cook, stirring occasionally, until fragrant, about 2 minutes.

Stir in cream; simmer until sauce is thick enough to coat back of spoon, about 5 minutes. Stir in basil.

NUTRITIONAL INFORMATION, PER ¼ CUP: about 246 cal, 2 g pro, 25 g total fat (14 g sat. fat), 5 g carb, 1 g fibre, 76 mg chol, 86 mg sodium, 193 mg potassium. % RDI: 5% calcium, 3% iron, 25% vit A, 47% vit C, 3% folate.

Wild Mushroom Cream Sauce

HANDS-ON TIME
15 MINUTES
•
TOTAL TIME
15 MINUTES
•
MAKES
1¼ CUPS

What you need

1 tbsp	butter
1	shallot, diced
2	cloves garlic, minced
2 cups	sliced mixed fresh mushrooms (such as cremini, shiitake and oyster)
½ cup	dry white wine
½ cup	whipping cream (35%)
pinch	each salt and pepper
1 tbsp	chopped fresh parsley

How to make it

In skillet, melt butter over medium heat; cook shallot, stirring, until softened, about 2 minutes. Add garlic; cook, stirring, for 1 minute.

Add mushrooms; cook over medium-high heat, stirring occasionally, until softened and no liquid remains, about 5 minutes. Add wine; reduce heat to simmer and cook for 4 minutes.

Add cream, salt and pepper; simmer until sauce is thick enough to coat back of spoon, about 2 minutes. Stir in parsley.

NUTRITIONAL INFORMATION, PER ¼ CUP: about 94 cal, 1 g pro, 8 g total fat (5 g sat. fat), 3 g carb, 1 g fibre, 26 mg chol, 27 mg sodium, 159 mg potassium. % RDI: 2% calcium, 3% iron, 8% vit A, 2% vit C, 3% folate.

**Tomato Red Pepper
Cream Sauce**
opposite

**Wild Mushroom
Cream Sauce**
opposite

Classic Marinara Sauce
page 104

Classic Marinara Sauce

HANDS-ON TIME
40 MINUTES

TOTAL TIME
40 MINUTES

MAKES
ABOUT 3 CUPS

What you need

1 tbsp	olive oil
1	onion, diced
1	clove garlic, chopped
1	can (796 mL) whole tomatoes
1 tbsp	balsamic vinegar
¼ tsp	granulated sugar
¼ cup	thinly sliced fresh basil (optional)

How to make it

In saucepan, heat oil over medium heat; cook onion, stirring occasionally, until golden, about 3 minutes. Add garlic; cook, stirring, until fragrant, about 1 minute.

Stir in tomatoes, vinegar and sugar, breaking up tomatoes with spoon; bring to boil. Reduce heat to simmer; cook, stirring often, until thickened, about 30 minutes.

Transfer sauce to food processor; purée until smooth. Stir in basil (if using). *(Make-ahead: Refrigerate in airtight container for up to 3 days.)*

VARIATION
Arrabbiata Sauce
Add ¼ tsp hot pepper flakes along with the garlic. If you like your sauce even spicier, increase to ½ tsp hot pepper flakes.

NUTRITIONAL INFORMATION, PER ¼ CUP: about 27 cal, 1 g pro, 1 g total fat (trace sat. fat), 4 g carb, 1 g fibre, 0 mg chol, 86 mg sodium, 142 mg potassium. % RDI: 2% calcium, 5% iron, 1% vit A, 15% vit C, 2% folate.

Slow Cooker Beef and Tomato Ragù

HANDS-ON TIME
25 MINUTES

TOTAL TIME
8½ HOURS

MAKES
ABOUT 7 CUPS

What you need

2 cups	bottled strained tomatoes (passata)
1	can (156 mL) tomato paste
2 tsp	balsamic vinegar
1 tsp	granulated sugar
1	each onion, carrot and rib celery, diced
¼ cup	diced thick pancetta
10	sprigs fresh thyme
2	bay leaves
2 tsp	dried oregano
¼ tsp	each salt, pepper and hot pepper flakes
900 g	boneless beef pot roast (top or bottom blade, or cross rib), trimmed

How to make it

In bowl, stir together strained tomatoes, tomato paste, vinegar and sugar; set aside. In slow cooker, combine onion, carrot, celery, pancetta, thyme, bay leaves, oregano, salt, pepper and hot pepper flakes. Add beef; pour tomato mixture over top. Cover and cook on low until beef is tender, 8 to 10 hours.

Discard thyme sprigs and bay leaves. Remove beef to cutting board; let cool slightly. Using 2 forks, shred into bite-size pieces; return to slow cooker, stirring to coat.

NUTRITIONAL INFORMATION, PER ¼ CUP: about 65 cal, 7 g pro, 3 g total fat (1 g sat. fat), 3 g carb, trace fibre, 17 mg chol, 104 mg sodium, 212 mg potassium. % RDI: 1% calcium, 9% iron, 6% vit A, 4% vit C, 2% folate.

Serve this chunky meat sauce over penne, rigatoni or pappardelle.

Slow Cooker Beef and Tomato Ragù
opposite

Classic Pesto

HANDS-ON TIME	TOTAL TIME	MAKES
5 MINUTES	5 MINUTES	ABOUT ¾ CUP

What you need

½ cup	grated Parmesan cheese
⅓ cup	pine nuts
2	cloves garlic
2½ cups	packed fresh basil
¼ tsp	each salt and pepper
⅓ cup	extra-virgin olive oil

How to make it

In food processor, pulse together Parmesan, pine nuts and garlic until coarsely ground. Add basil, salt and pepper; pulse 6 times.

With motor running, add oil in thin steady stream until smooth. *(Make-ahead: Refrigerate in airtight container for up to 3 days or freeze for up to 6 months.)*

NUTRITIONAL INFORMATION, PER 1 TBSP: about 99 cal, 2 g pro, 10 g total fat (2 g sat. fat), 1 g carb, trace fibre, 4 mg chol, 112 mg sodium, 60 mg potassium. % RDI: 5% calcium, 4% iron, 4% vit A, 2% vit C, 3% folate.

Cilantro, Chili and Sunflower Seed Pesto

HANDS-ON TIME	TOTAL TIME	MAKES
5 MINUTES	5 MINUTES	ABOUT 1 CUP

What you need

1	red finger chili pepper, seeded and chopped
½ cup	unsalted sunflower seeds, toasted
3	cloves garlic
1 cup	fresh cilantro
½ tsp	grated lime zest
pinch	salt
⅓ cup	light-tasting olive oil

How to make it

In food processor, pulse together chili pepper, sunflower seeds and garlic until coarsely ground. Add cilantro, lime zest and salt; pulse 6 times.

With motor running, add oil in thin steady stream until smooth. *(Make-ahead: Refrigerate in airtight container for up to 3 days or freeze for up to 6 months.)*

NUTRITIONAL INFORMATION, PER 1 TBSP: about 66 cal, 1 g pro, 7 g total fat (1 g sat. fat), 1 g carb, trace fibre, 0 mg chol, 1 mg sodium, 30 mg potassium. % RDI: 1% calcium, 1% iron, 1% vit A, 3% vit C, 5% folate.

Mint and Pistachio Pesto

HANDS-ON TIME 5 MINUTES • **TOTAL TIME** 5 MINUTES • **MAKES** ABOUT 1 CUP

What you need

½ cup	unsalted shelled pistachios
1	clove garlic
1 cup	each packed fresh mint and fresh parsley
pinch	each salt and pepper
⅓ cup	extra-virgin olive oil

How to make it

In food processor, pulse pistachios with garlic until coarsely ground. Add mint, parsley, salt and pepper; pulse 6 times.

With motor running, add oil in thin steady stream until smooth. *(Make-ahead: Refrigerate in airtight container for up to 3 days or freeze for up to 6 months.)*

NUTRITIONAL INFORMATION, PER 1 TBSP: about 64 cal, 1 g pro, 6 g total fat (1 g sat. fat), 2 g carb, 1 g fibre, 0 mg chol, 3 mg sodium, 78 mg potassium. % RDI: 2% calcium, 6% iron, 5% vit A, 10% vit C, 5% folate.

Sun-Dried Tomato and Almond Pesto

HANDS-ON TIME 5 MINUTES • **TOTAL TIME** 5 MINUTES • **MAKES** ABOUT 1 CUP

What you need

½ cup	slivered almonds
2	cloves garlic
1 cup	drained oil-packed sun-dried tomatoes
¼ tsp	each salt and pepper
⅓ cup	extra-virgin olive oil

How to make it

In food processor, pulse almonds with garlic until coarsely ground. Add tomatoes, salt and pepper; pulse until finely chopped.

With motor running, add oil in thin steady stream until smooth. *(Make-ahead: Refrigerate in airtight container for up to 3 days or freeze for up to 6 months.)*

NUTRITIONAL INFORMATION, PER 1 TBSP: about 75 cal, 1 g pro, 7 g total fat (1 g sat. fat), 2 g carb, 1 g fibre, 0 mg chol, 55 mg sodium, 133 mg potassium. % RDI: 1% calcium, 3% iron, 1% vit A, 12% vit C, 1% folate.

Vegetarian Singapore Noodles

HANDS-ON TIME
30 MINUTES

TOTAL TIME
30 MINUTES

MAKES
4 SERVINGS

What you need

225 g	dried rice vermicelli (1/32 inch/1 mm wide)
3 tbsp	sodium-reduced soy sauce
2 tsp	granulated sugar
2 tbsp	vegetable oil
2 cups	shredded napa cabbage
1½ cups	drained cubed firm tofu
1	sweet red pepper, thinly sliced
115 g	snow peas, trimmed and thinly sliced
4	green onions, thinly sliced
2	cloves garlic, minced
4 tsp	curry powder
1½ tsp	each ground cumin and ground coriander
¼ tsp	each salt and pepper
¼ cup	chopped unsalted peanuts (optional)

How to make it

Prepare noodles according to package instructions. Drain; set aside.

Meanwhile, in bowl, whisk together soy sauce, sugar and ¾ cup water. Set aside.

In wok or large nonstick skillet, heat oil over medium-high heat; stir-fry cabbage, tofu, red pepper, snow peas, green onions and garlic for 2 minutes. Add curry powder, cumin, coriander, salt and pepper; stir-fry for 1 minute.

Stir in soy sauce mixture; bring to boil. Stir in noodles, tossing to coat; stir-fry until tender, about 7 minutes. Sprinkle with peanuts (if using).

TIP FROM THE TEST KITCHEN
For a gluten-free variation, use wheat-free tamari instead of the soy sauce and check the packaging on all ingredients (such as peanuts) for gluten.

NUTRITIONAL INFORMATION, PER SERVING: about 444 cal, 18 g pro, 15 g total fat (2 g sat. fat), 61 g carb, 5 g fibre, 0 mg chol, 658 mg sodium, 478 mg potassium. % RDI: 20% calcium, 31% iron, 16% vit A, 117% vit C, 32% folate.

Singapore Noodles
opposite

Spicy Taiwanese-Style Noodles
page 139

Singapore Noodles

HANDS-ON TIME	**TOTAL TIME**	**MAKES**
30 MINUTES	50 MINUTES	4 TO 6 SERVINGS

What you need

225 g	pork tenderloin, trimmed
2 tbsp	sodium-reduced soy sauce
1 tsp	sesame oil
½ tsp	salt
¼ tsp	pepper
280 g	dried rice vermicelli (1⁄32 inch/1 mm wide)
4 tsp	vegetable oil
2	eggs, lightly beaten
225 g	jumbo shrimp (21 to 24 count), peeled and deveined
1	small onion, thinly sliced
half	sweet red pepper, thinly sliced
2	cloves garlic, minced
2	green onions, cut in 1½-inch (4 cm) lengths
2 tsp	curry powder
1 tsp	each turmeric and granulated sugar
2 cups	bean sprouts

How to make it

Cut pork into thin strips. In bowl, stir together pork, 2 tsp of the soy sauce, the sesame oil, a pinch of the salt and the pepper. Cover and refrigerate for 30 minutes. *(Make-ahead: Refrigerate for up to 24 hours.)*

Meanwhile, prepare noodles according to package instructions. Drain and rinse under cold water; drain well.

In wok or large nonstick skillet, heat 1 tsp of the vegetable oil over medium-high heat; cook eggs, stirring, just until set, about 1 minute. Scrape onto plate. Wipe out wok. Add 1 tsp of the remaining vegetable oil to wok; sauté shrimp over medium-high heat until pink and opaque throughout, about 2 minutes. Transfer to plate. Add 1 tsp of the remaining vegetable oil to wok; sauté pork mixture over medium-high heat until just a hint of pink remains inside, about 3 minutes. Transfer to plate.

Add remaining vegetable oil to wok; sauté onion, red pepper and garlic over medium-high heat until pepper is tender-crisp, about 2 minutes. Add noodles, egg, shrimp, pork, green onions, curry powder, turmeric, sugar and remaining soy sauce and salt. Cook, stirring and tossing, until well combined and heated through, about 3 minutes. Add bean sprouts; cook, stirring, until softened, about 1 minute.

NUTRITIONAL INFORMATION, PER EACH OF 6 SERVINGS:
about 330 cal, 19 g pro, 7 g total fat (1 g sat. fat), 46 g carb, 3 g fibre, 124 mg chol, 504 mg sodium, 328 mg potassium. % RDI: 4% calcium, 18% iron, 8% vit A, 37% vit C, 18% folate.

Spicy Ginger and Green Onion Noodle Salad With Grilled Chicken

HANDS-ON TIME	TOTAL TIME	MAKES
25 MINUTES	25 MINUTES	4 SERVINGS

What you need

2	boneless skinless chicken breasts (about 450 g)
¼ tsp	each salt and pepper
225 g	dried rice vermicelli (⅛ inch/3 mm wide), see tip, below
3 tbsp	vegetable oil
2 tbsp	minced fresh ginger
4	cloves garlic, minced
8	green onions, thinly sliced
4 tsp	lime juice
4 tsp	sodium-reduced soy sauce
2 tsp	liquid honey
½ tsp	Asian chili sauce (such as sriracha)
1	sweet red pepper, thinly sliced
1	large carrot, cut in matchsticks
half	English cucumber, chopped

How to make it

Sprinkle chicken with a pinch each of the salt and pepper. Place on greased grill over medium-high heat; close lid and grill, turning once, until no longer pink inside, about 12 minutes. Cover loosely; let stand for 5 minutes. Thinly slice crosswise.

Meanwhile, prepare noodles according to package instructions. Drain and rinse under cold water; drain well.

Meanwhile, in small saucepan, heat oil over medium heat; cook ginger and garlic, stirring, until fragrant, about 2 minutes. Stir in green onions and remaining salt and pepper; cook, stirring, until onions are softened, about 2 minutes. Remove from heat; stir in lime juice, soy sauce, honey and chili sauce.

In large bowl, toss together ginger mixture, noodles, red pepper, carrot and cucumber. Top with chicken.

TIP FROM THE TEST KITCHEN
Rice vermicelli and rice noodles come in a variety of widths. You can substitute wider or thinner noodles depending on your preference, but our recipes have matched up specific widths with the dishes they're best suited to.

NUTRITIONAL INFORMATION, PER SERVING: about 478 cal, 29 g pro, 13 g total fat (1 g sat. fat), 60 g carb, 4 g fibre, 66 mg chol, 446 mg sodium, 648 mg potassium. % RDI: 5% calcium, 12% iron, 51% vit A, 75% vit C, 21% folate.

Spicy Pork Noodle Stir-Fry

HANDS-ON TIME
25 MINUTES
•
TOTAL TIME
25 MINUTES
•
MAKES
2 SERVINGS

What you need

115 g	dried rice vermicelli (⅛ inch/3 mm wide)
2 tbsp	sodium-reduced soy sauce
2 tsp	chili garlic paste (such as sambal oelek), see tip, below
1½ tsp	seasoned rice vinegar
1 tsp	granulated sugar
1 tsp	sesame oil
pinch	salt
225 g	lean ground pork
1 tsp	vegetable oil
1 cup	sliced stemmed shiitake mushrooms
1 cup	coleslaw mix
½ cup	snow peas, trimmed and thinly sliced
2	green onions, thinly sliced
2	cloves garlic, minced
3 tbsp	chopped unsalted roasted peanuts

How to make it

Prepare noodles according to package instructions. Drain. Set aside.

Meanwhile, whisk together soy sauce, chili paste, vinegar, sugar, sesame oil, salt and ⅓ cup water. Set aside.

In wok or large nonstick skillet, cook pork over medium-high heat, stirring occasionally and breaking up with spoon, until no longer pink, about 5 minutes. Using slotted spoon, transfer pork to plate. Set aside.

Drain fat from wok; wipe clean. Add vegetable oil and mushrooms; stir-fry over medium-high heat until mushrooms are beginning to soften, about 2 minutes. Add coleslaw mix, snow peas, green onions and garlic; stir-fry for 2 minutes.

Stir in soy sauce mixture and noodles, tossing to combine. Stir-fry until tender, about 3 minutes. Sprinkle with peanuts.

TIP FROM THE TEST KITCHEN
There's only a small amount of chili paste in this dish, so it's not too fiery. If you prefer a milder taste, just omit it.

NUTRITIONAL INFORMATION, PER SERVING: about 588 cal, 30 g pro, 24 g total fat (6 g sat. fat), 63 g carb, 6 g fibre, 67 mg chol, 892 mg sodium, 617 mg potassium. % RDI: 7% calcium, 20% iron, 12% vit A, 28% vit C, 20% folate.

Serve this soup with a variety of garnishes. Try bean sprouts, fresh herbs, sliced chilies and lime wedges.

Rice Noodles

Slow Cooker Rare Beef Pho

HANDS-ON TIME	TOTAL TIME	MAKES
30 MINUTES	24½ HOURS	6 SERVINGS

What you need

2	onions (unpeeled), halved
¾ cup	chopped fresh ginger (unpeeled)
6	cloves garlic, crushed
2	cinnamon sticks
4	whole star anise
1 tsp	each coriander seeds and black peppercorns
2.25 kg	beef soup bones
1	carrot, chopped
1 tbsp	fish sauce
2	strips lime zest
1¼ tsp	salt
1	pkg (454 g) dried rice stick noodles (¼ inch/ 5 mm wide)
225 g	beef top sirloin grilling steak, very thinly sliced across the grain

How to make it

Arrange onions, ginger and garlic on foil-lined rimmed baking sheet; broil until slightly charred, 5 to 7 minutes. Transfer to slow cooker.

Meanwhile, in small skillet, toast cinnamon, star anise, coriander and peppercorns over medium-high heat, stirring occasionally, until fragrant, about 5 minutes; add to slow cooker. Add beef bones, carrot, fish sauce and lime zest. Stir in 10 cups water. Cover and cook on low for 24 hours.

Skim fat from surface. Strain stock through cheesecloth-lined fine-mesh sieve into large saucepan; discard solids. Skim any remaining fat. Bring to boil; stir in salt.

While stock is coming to boil, prepare noodles according to package instructions; drain. Divide noodles and steak among serving bowls; spoon hot stock over top.

NUTRITIONAL INFORMATION, PER SERVING: about 382 cal, 16 g pro, 5 g total fat (2 g sat. fat), 66 g carb, 3 g fibre, 22 mg chol, 880 mg sodium, 620 mg potassium. % RDI: 3% calcium, 14% iron, 7% folate.

Vegetable Pho

HANDS-ON TIME 25 MINUTES	**TOTAL TIME** 25 MINUTES
MAKES 4 SERVINGS	

What you need

2 tsp	vegetable oil
half	onion, thinly sliced
¾ tsp	five-spice powder
1 cup	thinly sliced stemmed shiitake mushrooms
2 tsp	grated fresh ginger
¼ tsp	salt
1	pkg (900 mL) sodium-reduced vegetable broth
1	carrot, cut in matchsticks
225 g	Shanghai bok choy, quartered
2 tsp	lime juice
340 g	dried rice stick noodles (¼ inch/5 mm wide)
155 g	extra-firm tofu, drained and thinly sliced (see tip, below)
pinch	hot pepper flakes (optional)

How to make it

In saucepan, heat oil over medium-high heat; cook onion and five-spice powder, stirring occasionally, until softened, about 3 minutes. Add mushrooms, ginger and salt; cook, stirring, for 2 minutes.

Add broth and 1½ cups water; bring to boil. Reduce heat to simmer; cook for 5 minutes.

Add carrot, bok choy and lime juice; cook until bok choy is slightly softened, about 1 minute.

Meanwhile, prepare noodles according to package instructions. Drain and rinse under cold water. Divide noodles among serving bowls. Top with tofu. Ladle hot broth and vegetables over top. Sprinkle with hot pepper flakes (if using).

TIP FROM THE TEST KITCHEN
Extra-firm tofu has the right texture for slicing and will hold up well in the soup. Use up any leftovers in stir-fries.

NUTRITIONAL INFORMATION, PER SERVING: about 421 cal, 10 g pro, 6 g total fat (1 g sat. fat), 80 g carb, 5 g fibre, 0 mg chol, 771 mg sodium, 500 mg potassium. % RDI: 14% calcium, 15% iron, 63% vit A, 35% vit C, 22% folate.

For a bolder heat, stir a squeeze of sriracha into the broth.

Gluten-Free Pad Thai

HANDS-ON TIME	•	TOTAL TIME	•	MAKES
25 MINUTES		25 MINUTES		4 TO 6 SERVINGS

What you need

half	pkg (454 g pkg) dried rice stick noodles (¼ inch/5 mm wide)
⅓ cup	ketchup
⅓ cup	sodium-reduced chicken broth
¼ cup	gluten-free fish sauce
3 tbsp	lime juice
2 tsp	granulated sugar
1 tsp	Asian chili sauce (such as sriracha)
¼ cup	vegetable oil or peanut oil
2	eggs, lightly beaten
225 g	large shrimp (31 to 40 count), peeled and deveined
280 g	boneless skinless chicken breasts, thinly sliced
4	shallots, thinly sliced
1	sweet red pepper, thinly sliced
4	cloves garlic, minced
2 tsp	minced fresh ginger
170 g	medium-firm tofu, drained and cubed
3 cups	bean sprouts
3	green onions, sliced
¼ cup	chopped unsalted roasted peanuts
½ cup	fresh cilantro
	lime wedges (optional)

How to make it

Prepare noodles according to package instructions. Drain. Set aside.

Meanwhile, in bowl, whisk together ketchup, broth, fish sauce, lime juice, sugar and chili sauce. Set aside.

In wok or large nonstick skillet, heat 1 tbsp of the oil over medium-high heat; cook eggs, stirring occasionally, until scrambled and set, about 30 seconds. Scrape into separate bowl.

Wipe out wok. Add 1 tbsp of the remaining oil and heat over high heat; stir-fry shrimp until pink and opaque throughout, about 1 minute. Transfer to plate.

Add 1 tbsp of the remaining oil to wok and heat over high heat; stir-fry chicken until browned and no longer pink inside, about 1 minute. Add to plate with shrimp.

Add remaining oil to wok and heat over high heat; cook shallots, red pepper, garlic and ginger, stirring, until softened, about 2 minutes. Stir in ketchup mixture and noodles. Return shrimp and chicken to wok; cook, stirring to coat, until noodles are tender, about 3 minutes.

Return eggs to wok; stir in tofu, bean sprouts and green onions. Cook just until bean sprouts begin to wilt, about 1 minute. Sprinkle with peanuts and cilantro. Serve with lime wedges (if using).

NUTRITIONAL INFORMATION, PER EACH OF 6 SERVINGS: about 453 cal, 28 g pro, 17 g total fat (3 g sat. fat), 47 g carb, 3 g fibre, 133 mg chol, 1,241 mg sodium, 555 mg potassium. % RDI: 11% calcium, 20% iron, 16% vit A, 73% vit C, 31% folate.

Cold Chicken Noodle Salad

HANDS-ON TIME	•	TOTAL TIME	•	MAKES
15 MINUTES		20 MINUTES		2 SERVINGS

What you need

NOODLE SAUCE:

1 tbsp	sodium-reduced soy sauce
1 tbsp	lime juice
1 tbsp	sesame oil
2 tsp	liquid honey
1 tsp	grated fresh ginger
1	clove garlic, finely grated or pressed
pinch	pepper

CHICKEN NOODLE SALAD:

225 g	boneless skinless chicken breast
pinch	each salt and pepper
85 g	dried rice vermicelli (⅛ inch/3 mm wide)
half	sweet red pepper, sliced
1 cup	matchstick-cut carrots
1 cup	diced English cucumber
1	green onion, chopped

How to make it

NOODLE SAUCE: In bowl, whisk together soy sauce, lime juice, sesame oil, honey, ginger, garlic and pepper. Set aside. (*Make-ahead: Refrigerate in airtight container for up to 2 days.*)

CHICKEN NOODLE SALAD: Sprinkle chicken with salt and pepper. Place on greased grill or in grill pan over medium heat; close lid and grill, turning once, until no longer pink inside, about 8 minutes. Let stand on cutting board for 5 minutes before slicing. (*Make-ahead: Cover and refrigerate for up to 2 days.*)

While chicken is grilling, prepare noodles according to package instructions. Drain and rinse under cold water; drain again. Set aside.

Divide noodles, red pepper, carrots, cucumber and chicken among serving bowls. Sprinkle with green onion. (*Make-ahead: Cover and refrigerate for up to 24 hours.*) Toss with Noodle Sauce.

NUTRITIONAL INFORMATION, PER SERVING: about 420 cal, 33 g pro, 10 g total fat (2 g sat. fat), 50 g carb, 5 g fibre, 67 mg chol, 518 mg sodium, 755 mg potassium. % RDI: 5% calcium, 21% iron, 113% vit A, 77% vit C, 57% folate.

Fried Rice Vermicelli

HANDS-ON TIME	•	**TOTAL TIME**	•	**MAKES**
30 MINUTES		35 MINUTES		4 TO 6 SERVINGS

What you need

1	pkg (300 g) dried rice vermicelli (1/32 inch/ 1 mm wide)
115 g	pork tenderloin, trimmed
170 g	medium shrimp (41 to 50 count), peeled and deveined
1 tsp	cornstarch
1 tsp	sake (Japanese rice wine)
1 tsp	salt
½ tsp	grated fresh ginger
2	eggs
pinch	white pepper
¼ cup	peanut oil or vegetable oil
half	onion, thinly sliced
2	cloves garlic, minced
2 tbsp	Madras curry powder (optional)
1¼ cups	chicken broth
1 cup	chopped Chinese chives or garlic chives (optional)
1 tbsp	soy sauce
2 cups	bean sprouts
1	green onion, thinly sliced
⅓ cup	fresh cilantro sprigs

How to make it

Prepare noodles according to package instructions. Drain. Set aside.

Cut pork into thin strips. In bowl, stir together pork, shrimp, cornstarch, sake, ½ tsp of the salt and the ginger; let stand for 10 minutes.

Meanwhile, in separate bowl, whisk together eggs, a pinch of the remaining salt, the pepper and 2 tbsp water. Set aside.

In wok or large nonstick skillet, heat 1 tbsp of the oil over medium-high heat; pour in egg mixture. Cook, swirling wok, to coat bottom with thin layer, until lightly set. Transfer to plate.

Add remaining oil to wok; stir-fry onion, garlic and curry powder (if using) until beginning to soften. Add pork mixture; stir-fry until shrimp are pink and opaque throughout. Add noodles, broth, chives (if using), soy sauce, remaining salt and eggs; stir-fry until eggs are broken up. Increase heat to high; add sprouts and stir-fry until noodles are tender and no liquid remains, about 3 minutes.

Add green onion; stir-fry for 30 seconds. Top with cilantro.

NUTRITIONAL INFORMATION, PER EACH OF 6 SERVINGS:
about 363 cal, 14 g pro, 12 g total fat (2 g sat. fat), 48 g carb, 3 g fibre, 106 mg chol, 826 mg sodium, 255 mg potassium. % RDI: 5% calcium, 15% iron, 4% vit A, 8% vit C, 17% folate.

Hanoi-Style Vermicelli Noodles With Fish

HANDS-ON TIME	TOTAL TIME	MAKES
25 MINUTES	1¼ HOURS	4 SERVINGS

What you need

How to make it

MARINATED FISH:

2	each shallots and cloves garlic, finely chopped
2 tbsp	chopped fresh dill
1 tbsp	each fish sauce, vinegar and vegetable oil
1½ tsp	minced fresh ginger
¾ tsp	turmeric
½ tsp	pepper
450 g	tilapia fillets

NOODLE SAUCE:

2 tbsp	granulated sugar
¼ cup	finely shredded carrot
2 tbsp	each fish sauce and lime juice
2 tsp	vinegar
1	Thai bird's-eye pepper, minced

PICKLED SHALLOTS:

3	shallots, thinly sliced in rings
1 tbsp	vinegar
¼ tsp	granulated sugar

NOODLES:

225 g	dried rice vermicelli (⅛ inch/3 mm wide)
2 cups	bean sprouts
1 cup	packed fresh cilantro
½ cup	coarsely chopped unsalted peanuts

MARINATED FISH: Using mortar and pestle, mash shallots with garlic to make paste. Stir in dill, fish sauce, vinegar, oil, ginger, turmeric, pepper and 1 tbsp water; spread all over fish. Cover and refrigerate for 1 hour.

On greased broiler pan, broil fish until browned and fish flakes easily when tested with fork, 8 to 10 minutes. Cut into portions.

NOODLE SAUCE: While fish is marinating, in heatproof bowl, whisk sugar with ⅔ cup hot water until dissolved; let cool. Stir in carrot, fish sauce, lime juice, vinegar and Thai pepper. Set aside.

PICKLED SHALLOTS: In separate bowl, stir together shallots, vinegar and sugar. Set aside.

NOODLES: Prepare noodles according to package instructions. Drain and rinse under cold water. Drain well; shake off excess liquid. Set aside to dry.

Divide noodles among serving dishes. Top with bean sprouts, cilantro, fish and pickled shallots; sprinkle with peanuts. Serve with Noodle Sauce.

NUTRITIONAL INFORMATION, PER SERVING: about 513 cal, 32 g pro, 15 g total fat (2 g sat. fat), 66 g carb, 5 g fibre, 50 mg chol, 1,145 mg sodium, 695 mg potassium. % RDI: 6% calcium, 16% iron, 14% vit A, 22% vit C, 35% folate.

Thai Chicken Noodle Bowl

HANDS-ON TIME
30 MINUTES

TOTAL TIME
30 MINUTES

MAKES
4 SERVINGS

What you need

1	stalk lemongrass, outer layers removed
2	slices (each 2 inches/5 cm) fresh ginger
2 cups	sodium-reduced chicken broth
1½ cups	thinly sliced stemmed shiitake mushrooms
1	red finger chili pepper, seeded and sliced
1 tbsp	packed brown sugar
1½ tsp	fish sauce
1 tsp	Thai red curry paste
1	can (400 mL) coconut milk
2 tbsp	cornstarch
half	sweet red pepper, sliced
125 g	dried rice stick noodles (¼-inch/5 mm wide)
2 cups	shredded skinless rotisserie chicken (white meat only)
⅓ cup	chopped fresh cilantro
1	green onion, sliced
2 tsp	lime juice

How to make it

Using back of large knife, bruise lemongrass and ginger. In large saucepan, bring lemongrass, ginger and broth to boil over medium-high heat. Stir in mushrooms and chili pepper; reduce heat to medium-low. Cook until mushrooms are tender, about 4 minutes.

Whisk together brown sugar, fish sauce and curry paste; stir into saucepan. Stir in coconut milk. Whisk cornstarch with 2 tbsp water; whisk into saucepan. Bring to simmer; cook until mixture is hot, fragrant and slightly thickened, about 3 minutes. Stir in sweet pepper; cook just until tender, about 1 minute. Discard lemongrass and ginger.

Meanwhile, prepare noodles according to package instructions. Drain; stir into saucepan. Add chicken, cilantro, green onion and lime juice; cook until heated through.

TIP FROM THE TEST KITCHEN

Bruising the lemongrass and ginger releases their flavours without breaking them into small pieces, making them easier to remove before serving.

NUTRITIONAL INFORMATION, PER SERVING: about 443 cal, 22 g pro, 23 g total fat (19 g sat. fat), 40 g carb, 3 g fibre, 50 mg chol, 701 mg sodium, 529 mg potassium. % RDI: 4% calcium, 28% iron, 6% vit A, 48 % vit C, 14% folate.

Rice Noodles With Pork

HANDS-ON TIME	•	TOTAL TIME	•	MAKES
30 MINUTES		30 MINUTES		6 SERVINGS

What you need

225 g	dried rice stick noodles (¼ inch/5 mm wide)
450 g	pork tenderloin, trimmed (see tip, below)
1 tbsp	cornstarch
3 tbsp	vegetable oil
half	onion, thinly sliced
3	cloves garlic, minced
2 tsp	minced fresh ginger
2 cups	thinly sliced cabbage
1	each carrot and sweet red pepper, thinly sliced
3 tbsp	sodium-reduced chicken broth or water
3 tbsp	sodium-reduced soy sauce
1 tbsp	each mild curry powder and granulated sugar
1 tbsp	tomato-based chili sauce
1 cup	bean sprouts

How to make it

Prepare noodles according to package instructions. Drain. Set aside.

Meanwhile, cut pork in half lengthwise. Sandwich between plastic wrap; using meat mallet or heavy-bottomed saucepan, pound to ½-inch (1 cm) thickness. Cut crosswise into strips. In bowl, toss together pork, cornstarch and 2 tbsp water; let stand for 10 minutes.

In wok or large nonstick skillet, heat half of the oil over medium-high heat; stir-fry pork until well browned but still pink inside, about 2 minutes. Using slotted spoon, transfer to plate.

Drain fat from wok; wipe clean. Add remaining oil; stir-fry onion, garlic and ginger over medium-high heat for 1 minute. Add cabbage, carrot and red pepper, stir-fry until tender-crisp, 2 to 4 minutes.

Whisk broth, soy sauce, curry powder, sugar and chili sauce; stir into wok. Add pork and any accumulated juices, bean sprouts and noodles; stir-fry until heated through.

TIP FROM THE TEST KITCHEN
Pork tenderloin is naturally lean, but sometimes it requires a little trimming. If you find any silverskin attached to the meat, make sure to remove it, as well.

NUTRITIONAL INFORMATION, PER SERVING: about 343 cal, 21 g pro, 9 g total fat (1 g sat. fat), 43 g carb, 3 g fibre, 45 mg chol, 430 mg sodium. % RDI: 3% calcium, 14% iron, 29% vit A, 68% vit C, 13% folate.

Beef and Pepper Black Bean Udon Noodles

HANDS-ON TIME	•	TOTAL TIME	•	MAKES
15 MINUTES		15 MINUTES		4 SERVINGS

What you need

2 tbsp	black bean garlic sauce
1 tsp	cornstarch
4 tsp	vegetable oil
450 g	beef flank marinating steak, cut crosswise in ⅛-inch (3 mm) thick slices
1	small onion, thinly sliced
1	sweet green pepper, thinly sliced
1	sweet red pepper, thinly sliced
1 tsp	minced fresh ginger
2	pkg (each 200 g) fresh udon noodles

How to make it

In small bowl, stir together black bean sauce, cornstarch and ½ cup water. Set aside.

In wok or large nonstick skillet, heat 2 tsp of the oil over medium-high heat; sauté steak until no longer pink, about 2 minutes. Using slotted spoon, transfer to plate.

Add remaining oil to wok; sauté onion, green pepper, red pepper and ginger until peppers are tender-crisp, about 2 minutes.

Meanwhile, in large saucepan of boiling water, cook noodles according to package instructions; drain.

Add steak, noodles and black bean mixture to wok; cook, stirring, until sauce is thickened, about 1 minute.

TIP FROM THE TEST KITCHEN

You can find fresh udon noodles in convenient 200 g packages in the Asian section of your supermarket. They cook quickly, making them a great addition to stir-fries and soups.

NUTRITIONAL INFORMATION, PER SERVING: about 406 cal, 30 g pro, 15 g total fat (4 g sat. fat), 38 g carb, 3 g fibre, 53 mg chol, 914 mg sodium, 489 mg potassium. % RDI: 3% calcium, 27% iron, 9% vit A, 118% vit C, 7% folate.

Stir-Fried Mongolian Noodles With Chicken

HANDS-ON TIME
20 MINUTES

•

TOTAL TIME
20 MINUTES

•

MAKES
4 SERVINGS

What you need

4 tsp	vegetable oil
2	boneless skinless chicken breasts (about 450 g total), thinly sliced crosswise
2	pkg (each 200 g) fresh udon noodles (see tip, page 129)
4 cups	broccoli florets
1 tbsp	hoisin sauce
1 tbsp	sodium-reduced soy sauce
¼ tsp	pepper
4	cloves garlic, minced
1	red finger chili pepper, thinly sliced

How to make it

In wok or large nonstick skillet, heat 1 tbsp of the oil over medium-high heat; stir-fry chicken until golden and no longer pink inside, about 5 minutes. Using slotted spoon, transfer to plate. Set aside.

Meanwhile, in large saucepan of boiling water, cook noodles and broccoli until noodles are tender and broccoli is tender-crisp, about 3 minutes; drain well.

In small bowl, stir together hoisin sauce, soy sauce, pepper and ⅓ cup water. Set aside.

In same wok, heat remaining oil over medium-high heat; stir-fry garlic and chili pepper until fragrant, about 30 seconds. Add noodle mixture, chicken and hoisin sauce mixture; stir-fry until coated and sauce is slightly thickened, about 2 minutes.

NUTRITIONAL INFORMATION, PER SERVING: about 486 cal, 35 g pro, 8 g total fat (2 g sat. fat), 64 g carb, 2 g fibre, 65 mg chol, 423 mg sodium, 601 mg potassium. % RDI: 6% calcium, 14% iron, 22% vit A, 73% vit C, 17% folate.

Freeze chicken breasts for
15 minutes to firm them up—
this makes slicing easier.

Soba Noodles

Chicken and Swiss Chard Noodle Stir-Fry

HANDS-ON TIME
20 MINUTES

TOTAL TIME
20 MINUTES

MAKES
4 SERVINGS

What you need

4 tsp	sodium-reduced soy sauce
1 tbsp	lime juice
2 tsp	sesame oil
2 tsp	vegetable oil
225 g	boneless skinless chicken breast, thinly sliced
1 tbsp	grated fresh ginger
3	cloves garlic, minced
8 cups	chopped stemmed Swiss chard (about 1 bunch)
1	sweet yellow pepper, sliced
170 g	soba noodles
4 cups	snow peas, trimmed
2 tsp	sesame seeds, toasted (see tip, below)

How to make it

In small bowl, whisk together soy sauce, lime juice and sesame oil. Set aside.

In wok or large nonstick skillet, heat vegetable oil over medium-high heat; stir-fry chicken, ginger and garlic, stirring often, until chicken is light golden, about 3 minutes.

Add Swiss chard and yellow pepper; stir-fry until chard begins to wilt, about 2 minutes.

Meanwhile, in large saucepan of boiling water, cook noodles according to package instructions; drain. Add to wok. Add snow peas and soy sauce mixture; stir-fry for 1 minute. Sprinkle with sesame seeds.

TIP FROM THE TEST KITCHEN
Toast sesame seeds in a small skillet over medium heat until golden and fragrant, about 3 minutes. Shake the skillet often and don't leave the stove—the tiny seeds can burn quickly.

NUTRITIONAL INFORMATION, PER SERVING: about 310 cal, 24 g pro, 7 g total fat (1 g sat. fat), 42 g carb, 5 g fibre, 33 mg chol, 417 mg sodium, 819 mg potassium. % RDI: 8% calcium, 29% iron, 47% vit A, 143% vit C, 20% folate.

Gluten-Free Orange Ginger Soba Noodles With Salmon

HANDS-ON TIME	•	TOTAL TIME	•	MAKES
30 MINUTES		30 MINUTES		4 SERVINGS

What you need

450 g	gluten-free soba noodles (see tip, below)
450 g	skinless salmon fillets
½ tsp	ground coriander
pinch	each salt and pepper
2 tbsp	vegetable oil
¼ tsp	grated orange zest
3 tbsp	orange juice
2 tbsp	gluten-free light tamari
¼ tsp	grated lime zest
1 tbsp	lime juice
2 tsp	grated fresh ginger
1 tsp	liquid honey
pinch	hot pepper flakes
1	clove garlic, crushed
1	pkg (142 g) baby spinach

How to make it

In large saucepan of boiling water, cook noodles according to package instructions. Drain and rinse under cold water; drain well. Set aside.

Meanwhile, sprinkle salmon with coriander, salt and pepper. In large nonstick skillet, heat 1 tbsp of the oil over medium heat; cook salmon, turning once, until fish flakes easily when tested, about 12 minutes. Transfer to cutting board; let cool enough to handle. Break into large bite-size pieces. Set aside.

Meanwhile, in small bowl, whisk together orange zest, orange juice, tamari, lime zest, lime juice, ginger, honey and hot pepper flakes. Set aside.

In same skillet, heat remaining oil over medium heat; cook garlic, turning occasionally, until golden, about 2 minutes. Discard garlic. Stir in spinach; cook, stirring, until wilted, about 1 minute.

Stir in noodles and orange zest mixture; toss to coat. Gently stir in salmon; cook, stirring gently, until heated through, about 5 minutes.

TIP FROM THE TEST KITCHEN
Many soba noodles are made from a mix of buckwheat flour and regular wheat flour. If gluten is a concern for you, make sure you buy gluten-free 100% buckwheat soba noodles for this dish. Look for them in health food stores.

NUTRITIONAL INFORMATION, PER SERVING: about 649 cal, 41 g pro, 18 g total fat (3 g sat. fat), 87 g carb, 5 g fibre, 55 mg chol, 658 mg sodium, 670 mg potassium. % RDI: 7% calcium, 26% iron, 37% vit A, 22% vit C, 50% folate.

Soba Noodles

Soba Noodles
With Pea Shoots and Shiitakes

HANDS-ON TIME	TOTAL TIME	MAKES
30 MINUTES	30 MINUTES	6 SERVINGS

What you need

225 g	soba noodles
1 tbsp	each sesame oil and vegetable oil
2	cloves garlic, minced
280 g	shiitake mushrooms, stemmed and sliced
340 g	snow pea shoots (about 8 cups), see tip, below
⅓ cup	light mayonnaise
¼ cup	sodium-reduced soy sauce
1 tbsp	unseasoned rice vinegar
1 tsp	granulated sugar
1 tsp	sambal oelek or hot sauce (optional)

How to make it

In large saucepan of boiling water, cook noodles according to package instructions. Drain and rinse under cold water; drain well. Transfer to large bowl.

In wok or large nonstick skillet, heat half each of the sesame oil and vegetable oil over medium-high heat; sauté garlic until fragrant, about 15 seconds. Add mushrooms; sauté until tender, about 4 minutes. Add to noodles.

In same wok, heat remaining vegetable oil and sesame oil over medium-high heat; stir-fry pea shoots until wilted and tender, 5 minutes. Add to noodle mixture.

Whisk together mayonnaise, soy sauce, vinegar, sugar and sambal oelek (if using); pour over noodle mixture, tossing to coat. Serve at room temperature or chilled.

TIP FROM THE TEST KITCHEN

Snow pea shoots, called *dau miu*, are popular in Chinese cooking. Look for them in Chinese grocery stores in the spring, when they are in season. If you can't find them, substitute sliced Shanghai bok choy.

NUTRITIONAL INFORMATION, PER SERVING: about 247 cal, 10 g pro, 10 g total fat (1 g sat. fat), 34 g carb, 4 g fibre, 5 mg chol, 523 mg sodium, 186 mg potassium. % RDI: 1% calcium, 8% iron, 21% vit A, 47% vit C, 18% folate.

Soba Noodles
With Spinach and Tofu

HANDS-ON TIME
25 MINUTES

TOTAL TIME
45 MINUTES

MAKES
4 SERVINGS

What you need

1	piece (about 4 inches/10 cm long) dried kelp (see tip, below)
1 cup	bonito flakes (see tip, below)
½ cup	mirin (Japanese sweet rice wine)
⅓ cup	sodium-reduced soy sauce
2 tbsp	granulated sugar
1 tbsp	sake (Japanese rice wine)
250 g	soba noodles
450 g	fresh spinach, trimmed
1	pkg (300 g) soft tofu, drained and cubed
2	green onions, thinly sliced diagonally
2 tbsp	thin strips nori seaweed (optional)
1 tbsp	sesame seeds, toasted (see tip, page 133)

How to make it

In saucepan, soak kelp in 2 cups water for 15 minutes. Bring just to boil over medium heat. Discard kelp. Stir in bonito flakes; bring to simmer and cook for 6 minutes. Add mirin, soy sauce, sugar and sake; return to boil. Strain through cheesecloth-lined fine-mesh sieve into heatproof bowl; let sauce cool completely.

While sauce is cooling, in large saucepan of boiling water, cook noodles according to package instructions. Drain and rinse under cold water; drain well. Shake off excess water; let dry for 10 minutes.

Meanwhile, in skillet, bring ¼ cup water to simmer; add spinach. Cover and cook, stirring occasionally, just until wilted. Drain, pressing out liquid with back of spoon.

In large bowl, toss together noodles, spinach and 1 cup of the sauce; divide among serving bowls. Top with tofu, green onions, nori (if using) and sesame seeds. Serve with remaining sauce.

TIP FROM THE TEST KITCHEN
Dried kelp is a common Japanese ingredient used to make flavourful stocks. Look for it in Asian grocery stores under its Japanese name, *konbu*. Look for the bonito (dried fish) flakes, nori seaweed and mirin there, too.

NUTRITIONAL INFORMATION, PER SERVING: about 369 cal, 20 g pro, 4 g total fat (1 g sat. fat), 64 g carb, 6 g fibre, 0 mg chol, 918 mg sodium, 725 mg potassium. % RDI: 22% calcium, 44% iron, 106% vit A, 18% vit C, 92% folate.

Enjoy salted edamame and a beer as an appetizer before digging in to these noodles.

Shrimp, Snow Pea and Cashew Stir-Fry

HANDS-ON TIME
20 MINUTES

•

TOTAL TIME
20 MINUTES

•

MAKES
4 SERVINGS

What you need

170 g	soba noodles
2 tbsp	soy sauce
1 tbsp	unseasoned rice vinegar
2 tsp	sesame oil
2	green onions, sliced
225 g	medium shrimp (41 to 50 count), peeled and deveined
1 tbsp	vegetable oil
1 tsp	grated fresh ginger
2	cloves garlic, finely grated or pressed
280 g	snow peas, trimmed
½ cup	unsalted roasted cashews

How to make it

In large saucepan of boiling water, cook noodles according to package instructions. Drain and rinse under cold water; drain well. Set aside.

Meanwhile, in bowl, whisk together soy sauce, vinegar, sesame oil and green onions. Add shrimp, tossing to coat. Set aside.

In wok or large nonstick skillet, heat vegetable oil over high heat; stir-fry ginger and garlic until fragrant, about 30 seconds. Add snow peas; cook until slightly tender, 3 to 4 minutes.

Scrape shrimp mixture into wok: stir-fry until shrimp are pink and opaque throughout, 2 to 3 minutes. Add noodles and toss until heated through, about 1 minute. Sprinkle with cashews.

TIP FROM THE TEST KITCHEN
If you like chilies, add ¼ tsp hot pepper flakes along with the ginger and garlic.

NUTRITIONAL INFORMATION, PER SERVING: about 372 cal, 22 g pro, 14 g total fat (2 g sat. fat), 43 g carb, 4 g fibre, 65 mg chol, 607 mg sodium, 454 mg potassium. % RDI: 7% calcium, 31% iron, 10% vit A, 62% vit C, 20% folate.

Spicy Taiwanese-Style Noodles

HANDS-ON TIME
30 MINUTES

•

TOTAL TIME
30 MINUTES

•

MAKES
4 SERVINGS

What you need

1½ cups	sodium-reduced beef broth
2 tbsp	oyster sauce
4 tsp	cornstarch
1 tbsp	balsamic vinegar
2 tsp	granulated sugar
2 tsp	Asian chili sauce (such as sriracha)
pinch	five-spice powder
1 tbsp	vegetable oil
450 g	lean ground pork
2	cloves garlic, minced
1 tbsp	minced fresh ginger
2 cups	thinly sliced stemmed shiitake mushrooms
½ cup	coarsely chopped drained canned bamboo shoots
2	green onions, thinly sliced
340 g	dried Chinese wheat noodles or fresh steamed chow mein noodles

How to make it

In bowl, stir together broth, oyster sauce, cornstarch, vinegar, sugar, chili sauce and five-spice powder. Set aside.

In wok or large nonstick skillet, heat 1 tsp of the oil over medium-high heat; cook pork, stirring and breaking up with spoon, until no longer pink, about 4 minutes. Scrape into bowl.

Add remaining oil to wok; sauté garlic and ginger over medium-high heat until fragrant, about 30 seconds. Add mushrooms and bamboo shoots; cook, stirring occasionally, until mushrooms are softened, about 3 minutes. Add broth mixture, pork and green onions; cook, stirring, until sauce is thickened, about 2 minutes.

Meanwhile, in large saucepan of boiling water, cook noodles according to package instructions; drain. Divide among serving dishes; top with pork mixture.

TIP FROM THE TEST KITCHEN
The cooked noodles tend to stick together if they stand for a while. Mix the sauce into them and eat them right away for the best texture.

NUTRITIONAL INFORMATION, PER SERVING: about 635 cal, 35 g pro, 23 g total fat (7 g sat. fat), 73 g carb, 4 g fibre, 88 mg chol, 752 mg sodium, 507 mg potassium. % RDI: 5% calcium, 41% iron, 1% vit A, 3% vit C, 6% folate.

Korean Cold Somen Noodle Salad

HANDS-ON TIME
20 MINUTES
•
TOTAL TIME
45 MINUTES
•
MAKES
4 TO 6 SERVINGS

What you need

PICKLED DAIKON:

½ cup	thinly sliced peeled daikon radish
1 tbsp	unseasoned rice vinegar
½ tsp	granulated sugar

HOT PEPPER SAUCE:

3 tbsp	Korean hot pepper paste (gochujang)
3 tbsp	unseasoned rice vinegar
2 tbsp	sesame seeds, toasted (see tip, page 133)
2 tbsp	sesame oil
4 tsp	granulated sugar
1 tbsp	sodium-reduced soy sauce

SOMEN NOODLE SALAD:

275 g	somen noodles
half	English cucumber, halved lengthwise, seeded and sliced
115 g	sliced deli ham (optional), cut in strips
1½ cups	sliced cored Asian pear
1 cup	kimchi, chopped
½ cup	finely chopped green onions
¼ cup	kimchi juice
4 cups	shredded frisée or red leaf lettuce
1	sheet toasted nori, cut in strips

How to make it

PICKLED DAIKON: In bowl, stir together daikon, vinegar and sugar; cover and refrigerate for 15 minutes.

HOT PEPPER SAUCE: While daikon is chilling, in separate bowl, stir together hot pepper paste, vinegar, sesame seeds, sesame oil, sugar and soy sauce. Set aside.

SOMEN NOODLE SALAD: In large saucepan of boiling water, cook noodles according to package instructions. Drain and rinse under cold water until no longer starchy; drain well. Shake off excess liquid; let dry for 10 minutes.

In large bowl, combine noodles, cucumber, ham (if using), pear, kimchi, green onions and kimchi juice; add half of the Hot Pepper Sauce and toss to combine.

Add frisée; toss gently to coat. Sprinkle with nori. Divide among serving bowls; top with Pickled Daikon. Serve with remaining Hot Pepper Sauce.

NUTRITIONAL INFORMATION, PER EACH OF 6 SERVINGS:
about 257 cal, 6 g pro, 7 g total fat (1 g sat. fat), 43 g carb, 6 g fibre, 0 mg chol, 908 mg sodium, 269 mg potassium. % RDI: 4% calcium, 12% iron, 22% vit A, 23% vit C, 30% folate.

Making kimchi juice is easy.
Just squeeze the kimchi and top it
up with some brine from the jar.

Braised Chinese Beef and Daikon With Noodles

HANDS-ON TIME
40 MINUTES

•

TOTAL TIME
3¾ HOURS

•

MAKES
8 SERVINGS

What you need

¼ cup	all-purpose flour
2 tsp	ground coriander
½ tsp	pepper
¼ tsp	five-spice powder
pinch	salt
900 g	boneless beef brisket pot roast, cut in 1-inch (2.5 cm) chunks
2 tbsp	vegetable oil
6	cloves garlic, minced
1 tbsp	minced fresh ginger
¼ cup	Chinese rice wine
1½ cups	sodium-reduced beef broth
1 tsp	granulated sugar
2	whole star anise
1	cinnamon stick (3½ inches/9 cm long)
340 g	daikon radish, peeled and cut in 1-inch (2.5 cm) chunks (about 4½ cups)
2 tbsp	oyster sauce
4	green onions, cut in 1½-inch (4 cm) lengths
680 g	fresh steamed chow mein noodles or fresh Chinese wheat noodles

How to make it

In bowl, stir together 2 tbsp of the flour, the coriander, pepper, five-spice powder and salt; add beef and toss to coat.

In Dutch oven or large heavy-bottomed saucepan, heat oil over medium-high heat; working in batches, cook brisket, stirring, until browned, about 5 minutes per batch. Using slotted spoon, transfer to plate.

Add garlic and ginger to Dutch oven; sauté over medium-high heat until fragrant, about 30 seconds. Stir in wine, scraping up browned bits. Add broth, sugar, star anise, cinnamon stick, beef and ¾ cup water; bring to boil. Reduce heat; cover and simmer gently until beef is tender, about 2½ hours.

Stir in daikon; bring to boil. Reduce heat and simmer, uncovered, until tender, about 30 minutes.

Whisk together oyster sauce, remaining flour and 1 tbsp water; stir into beef mixture. Cook, stirring, until sauce is thickened, about 5 minutes. Stir in green onions; cook for 1 minute.

Meanwhile, in large saucepan of boiling water, cook noodles according to package instructions; drain. Divide among serving plates; top with beef mixture.

NUTRITIONAL INFORMATION, PER SERVING: about 652 cal, 33 g pro, 27 g total fat (9 g sat. fat), 70 g carb, 3 g fibre, 92 mg chol, 491 mg sodium, 480 mg potassium. % RDI: 5% calcium, 48% iron, 1% vit A, 12% vit C, 10% folate.

Wheat Noodles With Steamed Chicken and Sesame Mustard Sauce

HANDS-ON TIME	•	TOTAL TIME	•	MAKES
20 MINUTES		40 MINUTES		4 SERVINGS

What you need

SESAME MUSTARD SAUCE:

¼ cup	sesame seeds, toasted (see tip, page 133)
1½ tsp	granulated sugar
⅔ cup	mayonnaise
¼ cup	hot mustard
7 tsp	seasoned rice vinegar
2 tbsp	sodium-reduced soy sauce

NOODLES:

3	boneless skinless chicken breasts (about 565 g)
2 tbsp	sake (Japanese rice wine)
½ tsp	salt
400 g	dried Japanese or Chinese wheat noodles or linguine
1 tsp	sesame oil
1 cup	matchstick-cut carrots
half	English cucumber, cut in matchsticks
1 cup	bean sprouts
½ cup	frozen shelled edamame, thawed

How to make it

SESAME MUSTARD SAUCE: In food processor, pulse sesame seeds with sugar until finely ground. Add mayonnaise, mustard, vinegar and soy sauce; blend until smooth. Set aside.

NOODLES: Place rack or steamer in wok or large shallow pan; pour in enough water to come 1 inch (2.5 cm) below rack. Cover and bring to boil; reduce heat to medium-high. Place chicken on plate; sprinkle with sake and salt. Place on rack; cover and steam until no longer pink inside, about 15 minutes. Remove from steamer; drain and let cool. Slice diagonally into strips.

While chicken is steaming, in large saucepan of boiling water, cook noodles according to package instructions. Drain and rinse under cold water; drain well. Shake off excess liquid; let dry for 10 minutes. Toss with sesame oil.

Divide noodles among serving bowls; top with chicken, carrots, cucumber, bean sprouts and edamame. Serve with Sesame Mustard Sauce.

NUTRITIONAL INFORMATION, PER SERVING: about 846 cal, 46 g pro, 40 g total fat (6 g sat. fat), 74 g carb, 4 g fibre, 97 mg chol, 1,314 mg sodium, 775 mg potassium. % RDI: 8% calcium, 23% iron, 41% vit A, 13% vit C, 40% folate.

Shrimp Lo Mein

HANDS-ON TIME
20 MINUTES

•

TOTAL TIME
20 MINUTES

•

MAKES
4 SERVINGS

What you need

1 cup	sodium-reduced chicken broth
2 tbsp	oyster sauce
1 tbsp	cornstarch
1 tsp	sesame oil
1 tbsp	vegetable oil
450 g	jumbo shrimp (21 to 24 count), peeled and deveined
280 g	fresh steamed chow mein noodles
1	carrot, sliced on the diagonal
1 cup	snow peas, trimmed and halved diagonally
1 cup	quartered button or cremini mushrooms
3	cloves garlic, minced
3	heads Shanghai bok choy (about 225 g), quartered

How to make it

In bowl, stir together broth, oyster sauce, cornstarch and sesame oil. Set aside.

In wok or large nonstick skillet, heat 1 tsp of the vegetable oil over medium-high heat; sauté shrimp until pink and opaque throughout, about 2 minutes. Using slotted spoon, transfer to plate.

In large saucepan of boiling water, cook noodles according to package instructions. Drain. Set aside.

While noodles are cooking, add remaining oil to wok; sauté carrot, snow peas, mushrooms and garlic over medium-high heat until garlic is fragrant, about 1 minute. Add bok choy; sauté just until wilted, about 1 minute.

Stir in broth mixture, shrimp and noodles. Cook, tossing, until sauce is thickened and noodles are coated, about 1 minute.

VARIATION

Tofu Lo Mein

Omit shrimp. Reduce vegetable oil to 2 tsp; use to cook vegetables only. Add 450 g fried tofu balls to wok along with broth mixture. (Look for tofu balls in the refrigerated section of the grocery store near the wonton wrappers and tofu.)

NUTRITIONAL INFORMATION, PER SERVING: about 361 cal, 27 g pro, 7 g total fat (1 g sat. fat), 46 g carb, 3 g fibre, 132 mg chol, 646 mg sodium, 578 mg potassium. % RDI: 11% calcium, 36% iron, 63% vit A, 42% vit C, 19% folate.

Black Bean Beef and Asparagus

HANDS-ON TIME
30 MINUTES

•

TOTAL TIME
30 MINUTES

•

MAKES
4 SERVINGS

What you need

6	green onions
1	bunch (about 450 g) asparagus, trimmed
450 g	lean ground beef
340 g	dried Japanese or Chinese wheat noodles, or linguine
2 tbsp	vegetable oil
3	cloves garlic, minced
2 tsp	grated fresh ginger
1	Thai bird's-eye pepper (optional), minced
2 tbsp	black bean garlic sauce
⅓ cup	sodium-reduced chicken broth
2 tbsp	dry sherry (optional)
1 tbsp	sodium-reduced soy sauce
2 tsp	each granulated sugar and cornstarch
half	English cucumber, cut in 2-inch (5 cm) long sticks

How to make it

Separate light and dark green parts of green onions. Mince light parts. Cut 3 of the dark parts into 2-inch (5 cm) lengths; reserve remaining dark green parts for another use. Set aside.

In saucepan of boiling water, cook asparagus until tender-crisp, 3 to 5 minutes. Drain; cut into 2-inch (5 cm) lengths. Place beef in colander; lower colander into boiling water and cook for 1 minute. Drain. Set aside.

Meanwhile, in large saucepan of boiling water, cook noodles according to package instructions. Drain and rinse under cold water; drain well. Shake off excess liquid; let dry for 10 minutes.

While noodles are drying, in wok or large nonstick skillet, heat oil over medium-high heat; stir-fry garlic, light parts of green onions, ginger, Thai pepper (if using) and beef until fragrant and no liquid remains, about 5 minutes. Add black bean sauce; stir-fry for 1 minute.

Whisk together broth, sherry (if using), soy sauce, sugar, cornstarch and ½ cup water; add to wok. Add asparagus and dark parts of green onions; cook, stirring, until thickened, glossy and asparagus is heated through. Add noodles and toss to coat. Top with cucumber.

NUTRITIONAL INFORMATION, PER SERVING: about 786 cal, 34 g pro, 39 g total fat (13 g sat. fat), 75 g carb, 8 g fibre, 155 mg chol, 613 mg sodium. % RDI: 8% calcium, 34% iron, 11% vit A, 17% vit C, 70% folate.

Ground beef cooks faster
than cubed beef, so it's a stir-fry
time-saver.

Tofu Noodle Stir-Fry

| HANDS-ON TIME 20 MINUTES | • | TOTAL TIME 20 MINUTES | • | MAKES 4 SERVINGS |

What you need

1	pkg (425 g) firm tofu, drained
2 tbsp	sodium-reduced soy sauce
1 tbsp	sesame oil
2 tsp	vegetable oil
1 cup	frozen green peas
¾ cup	finely chopped green onions
2 tbsp	grated fresh ginger
2	cloves garlic, minced
1 cup	vegetable broth
280 g	fresh steamed chow mein noodles
⅓ cup	chopped roasted cashews

How to make it

Pat tofu dry; cut into ½-inch (1 cm) cubes. In bowl, whisk together half each of the soy sauce and sesame oil; add tofu and toss to coat.

In wok or large nonstick skillet, heat vegetable oil over medium-high heat; stir-fry tofu until light golden and crisp, about 5 minutes. Using slotted spoon, transfer to plate.

Add peas, green onions, ginger, garlic and remaining soy sauce to wok; stir-fry over medium-high heat for 2 minutes. Stir in broth and bring to boil; cook for 2 minutes.

Meanwhile, in large saucepan of boiling water, cook noodles according to package instructions. Drain; add to wok. Add tofu; stir-fry until noodles are coated and tofu is heated through, about 2 minutes. Stir in remaining sesame oil; sprinkle with cashews.

NUTRITIONAL INFORMATION, PER SERVING: about 482 cal, 27 g pro, 20 g total fat (3 g sat. fat), 52 g carb, 3 g fibre, 5 mg chol, 635 mg sodium, 407 mg potassium. % RDI: 18% calcium, 38% iron, 9% vit A, 10% vit C, 24% folate.

Beef Ramen Soup

HANDS-ON TIME	•	TOTAL TIME	•	MAKES
25 MINUTES		35 MINUTES		4 SERVINGS

What you need

340 g	beef top sirloin grilling steak
¼ tsp	each salt and pepper
4	pkg (each 100 g) instant ramen noodles
1 tbsp	vegetable oil
2	green onions (light and dark green parts separated), thinly sliced
2	cloves garlic, thinly sliced
2	slices fresh ginger
225 g	shiitake mushrooms, stemmed and thinly sliced
4 cups	sodium-reduced beef broth
3 tbsp	teriyaki sauce
1	carrot, cut in matchsticks
1 cup	bean sprouts

How to make it

Sprinkle steak with salt and pepper. In greased grill pan or heavy-bottomed skillet, cook steak over medium-high heat, turning once, until medium-rare, about 6 minutes, or until desired doneness. Transfer to cutting board and cover loosely with foil; let rest for 10 minutes. Thinly slice across the grain.

Meanwhile, fill Dutch oven with water; bring to boil. Cook noodles (discarding spice packets) according to package instructions. Drain; divide among serving bowls.

In same Dutch oven, heat oil over medium-high heat; sauté light parts of green onions, garlic, ginger and mushrooms until softened, about 3 minutes. Add broth and 4 cups water; bring to boil. Whisk in teriyaki sauce; reduce heat to simmer and cook for 10 minutes.

Add carrot; cook for 1 minute. Ladle soup over noodles. Add beef and bean sprouts; sprinkle with dark parts of green onions.

NUTRITIONAL INFORMATION, PER SERVING: about 636 cal, 33 g pro, 25 g total fat (10 g sat. fat), 70 g carb, 7 g fibre, 40 mg chol, 1,343 mg sodium. % RDI: 6% calcium, 29% iron, 33% vit A, 10% vit C, 24% folate.

Japchae

HANDS-ON TIME		TOTAL TIME		MAKES
25 MINUTES	•	25 MINUTES	•	4 SERVINGS

What you need

280 g	sweet potato vermicelli
2 tbsp	sodium-reduced soy sauce
5 tsp	sesame oil
1 tsp	granulated sugar
2	cloves garlic, minced
1	carrot, cut in matchsticks
2 cups	sliced stemmed shiitake mushrooms
1	sweet red pepper, thinly sliced
5	green onions, cut in 1½-inch (4 cm) lengths
1	bunch fresh spinach, stemmed and chopped (about 4 cups)
2 tsp	sesame seeds, toasted (see tip, page 133)

How to make it

In large saucepan of boiling water, cook noodles according to package instructions; drain. Using kitchen shears, cut into shorter lengths; toss with 2 tsp each of the soy sauce and sesame oil.

Meanwhile, in large bowl, stir together remaining soy sauce, 2 tsp of the remaining sesame oil and the sugar. Set aside.

In wok or large nonstick skillet, heat remaining sesame oil over medium-high heat; sauté garlic until fragrant, about 1 minute. Add carrot, mushrooms, red pepper and green onions; sauté until pepper is tender-crisp, about 2 minutes. Add spinach; sauté just until wilted, about 1 minute. Remove from heat.

Add noodles and carrot mixture to soy sauce mixture. Sprinkle with sesame seeds.

TIP FROM THE TEST KITCHEN

The sweet potato vermicelli are long, so cutting them with kitchen shears makes the noodles easier (and more enjoyable) to eat.

NUTRITIONAL INFORMATION, PER SERVING: about 348 cal, 6 g pro, 7 g total fat (1 g sat. fat), 67 g carb, 4 g fibre, 0 mg chol, 356 mg sodium, 425 mg potassium. % RDI: 9% calcium, 21% iron, 72% vit A, 92% vit C, 30% folate.

THANK YOU!

Like everyone else, it seems, I love pasta. So working with a phenomenal team to create a book on this topic was especially fun. From choosing the first mouthwatering recipes to typing in the final corrections, it's been a pleasure to work with the people who made this book.

First, I'd like to thank food director Annabelle Waugh, senior food specialist Irene Fong and food specialists Amanda Barnier, Jennifer Bartoli and Gilean Watts. From the sublime (inventing, tasting and critiquing recipes) to the seemingly ridiculous (weighing individual capers so our nutrient analysis is ultra-precise), these women do anything and everything in their power to ensure Canadian Living's recipes are Tested Till Perfect. They're consummate pros and wonderful people to work with.

Second, I'd like to give thanks to our art director, Colin Elliott. Whether he's creating new and exciting layouts or checking fractions of an inch on printer specifications, he's a pro, too. His creativity and knowledge make our books beautiful and practical at the same time.

Next, a big thank-you to the talented photographers and stylists who created the beautiful photos. Special thanks to photographer Jeff Coulson, food stylist Bernadette Ammar and prop stylist Sasha Seymour for the fresh new images they created for this cookbook. For a complete list of the photographers and stylists who contributed to these pages, see right.

Thanks to Gilean Watts for doing double duty as copy editor. She cleaned up my grammatical errors and made this book much clearer in the process. Thanks as well to indexer Beth Zabloski for organizing the handy index starting on page 153 so you can easily find the information you're looking for. Thanks also to Sharyn Joliat of Info Access, who created the helpful nutrient analysis for all of our recipes.

Merci beaucoup to the teams at Juniper Publishing and Simon & Schuster Canada for helping us promote and distribute this book across the country. They are another top-notch group of professionals, and we enjoy working with them on each new project.

Finally, a big thanks to Canadian Living's group publisher, Sandra E. Martin, and content director, multiplatform editions, special issues and books, Jessica Ross, for their hard work and great ideas on this and many other projects.

TINA ANSON MINE
PROJECT EDITOR

RECIPES
All recipes Tested Till Perfect by the Canadian Living Test Kitchen

PHOTOGRAPHY
Ryan Brook: back cover (food, left centre); p. 114 and 148.
Jeff Coulson: back cover (food, all except left centre); p. 5, 6, 10, 14, 17, 23, 26, 48, 53, 57, 61, 64, 73, 76, 79, 85, 91, 98, 105, 110, 113, 116, 120, 128, 131, 132, 141 and 145.
André Doyon: p. 35.
Yvonne Duivenvoorden: front cover; p. 41, 68, 109 and 119.
Joe Kim: p. 67.
Edward Pond: p. 82.
Jodi Pudge: p. 31, 45, 125 and 137.
David Scott: p. 18, 95 and 146.
Shoot Studio: p. 42 and 74.
Ryan Szulc: p. 54 and 103.
Tango Photographie: p. 92.

FOOD STYLING
Bernadette Ammar: p. 10, 14, 23, 26 and 48.
Stéphan Boucher: p. 42 and 74.
Ashley Denton: p. 54, 67 and 103.
Anne Gagné: p. 35.
Véronique Gagnon-Lalanne: p. 92.
David Grenier: back cover (left centre, right); p. 61, 85, 113, 114, 120 and 131.
Adele Hagan: p. 64.
Lucie Richard: front cover; p. 18, 31, 68, 95, 109 and 146.
Claire Stubbs: back cover (left top, centre); p. 17, 41, 45, 53, 57, 73, 82, 91, 125, 132 and 137.
Melanie Stuparyk: back cover (left bottom); p. 6, 76, 98, 116 and 148.
Noah Witenoff: p. 105, 110, 128 and 145.
LeeAnne Wright: p. 5 and 79.
Nicole Young: p. 119 and 141.

PROP STYLING
Laura Branson: back cover (left centre); p. 18, 54, 64, 103, 114 and 148.
Aurelie Bryce: back cover (right); p. 5, 61, 79, 85 and 105.
Catherine Doherty: p. 45, 57, 67, 82, 91, 119, 120, 125, 137 and 141.
Véronique Gagnon-Lalanne: p. 92.
Mandy Gyulay: p. 68 and 109.
Madeleine Johari: back cover (all except left centre and right) p. 6, 17, 41, 53, 73, 76, 98, 110, 128, 132 and 145.
Sabrina Linn: p. 116.
Sasha Seymour: p. 10, 14, 23, 26, 48, 113 and 131.
Caroline Simon: p. 35, 42 and 74.
Oksana Slavutych: p. 95 and 146.
Genevieve Wiseman: front cover; p. 31.

INDEX

V = Vegetarian

v = Vegetarian

Index

v = Vegetarian

Index

v = Vegetarian

About Our Nutrition Information

To meet nutrient needs each day, moderately active women aged 25 to 49 need about 1,900 calories, 51 g protein, 261 g carbohydrate, 25 to 35 g fibre and not more than 63 g total fat (21 g saturated fat). Men and teenagers usually need more. Canadian sodium intake of approximately 3,500 mg daily should be reduced, whereas the intake of potassium from food sources should be increased to 4,700 mg per day. The percentage of recommended daily intake (% RDI) is based on the values used for Canadian food labels for calcium, iron, vitamins A and C, and folate.

Figures are rounded off. They are based on the first ingredient listed when there is a choice and do not include optional ingredients or those with no specified amounts.

ABBREVIATIONS

cal = calories

pro = protein

carb = carbohydrate

sat. fat = saturated fat

chol = cholesterol

Canadian Living

Complete your collection of Tested-Till-Perfect recipes!

Canadian Living: The Ultimate Cookbook

150 Essential Beef, Pork & Lamb Recipes
150 Essential Salads
150 Essential Whole Grain Recipes

New Slow Cooker Favourites

400-Calorie Dinners
Dinner in 30 Minutes or Less
Make It Chocolate!
Pasta & Noodles
Sweet & Simple

The Affordable Feasts Collection
The Appetizer Collection
The Barbecue Collection
The International Collection
The One Dish Collection
The Slow Cooker Collection
The Vegetarian Collection

The Complete Chicken Book
The Complete Chocolate Book
The Complete Preserving Book